INSIDE THE WEST WING

An Unauthorized Look at
Television's Smartest Show

PAUL CHALLEN

ECW PRESS

NATIONAL LIBRARY OF CANADA CATALOGUING IN PUBLICATION DATA

Challen Paul C. (Paul Clarence), 1967–
Inside the West Wing

ISBN 1-55022-468-9

1. West Wing (Television program) I. Title.

PN1992.77.W48C45   2001   791.45'72   C2001-900807-4

Cover and text design by Tania Craan
Front cover: cast photo by Ron Davis: Shooting Star; White House and flag: Firstlight
Layout by Mary Bowness

Printed by AGMV

Distributed in Canada by
General Distribution Services,
325 Humber College Blvd.,
Toronto, ON   M9W 7C3

Distributed in the United States by
LPC Group
1436 West Randolph Street,
Chicago, IL   USA   60607

Published by ECW PRESS
2120 Queen Street East, Suite 200
Toronto, ON   M4E 1E2
ecwpress.com

This book is set in Minion and Centaur.

PRINTED AND BOUND IN CANADA

The publication of *Inside the West Wing* has been generously supported by the Canada Council,
the Ontario Arts Council and the Government of Canada through the
Book Publishing Industry Development Program. Canada

CONTENTS

ACKNOWLEDGEMENTS

I'd like to thank many people for their assistance in compiling this look at *The West Wing*:

Jack David, Jen Hale and Richard Bowness at ECW Press;

My agent — and big time fan of *The West Wing* — Don Sedgwick;

The Television Critics Association for access to interview and press conference material, and especially to Eric Kohanik, past TCA president and editor of *TV Times* and *Post-TV* magazines, for his insights and help in general;

Web site creators B.E. Warne, Susannah Nix, Rachel Vagts, and Lesley Gayle for their invaluable insight into the fan's perspective on the show;

Tad Friend of the *New Yorker* magazine;

John Harris and John Maynard of the *Washington Post*;

My parents Paul and Cecilia Challen for their expert VCR work on Wednesday nights;

My wife Janine Belzak and our kids Sam, Eva, and Henry for their unflagging support and constant good cheer;

And, above all, to Aaron Sorkin, John Wells, Tommy Schlamme, and the cast of *The West Wing*, North America's smartest TV show.

Disclaimer: This is an unauthorized book about *The West Wing*, and as such, was written without the consent of Warner Brothers Studios or the NBC Television Network. Wherever possible, care has been taken to cite the sources of quoted material within the text; for a full list of sources used in compiling this book, see "Sources," page 181.

All errors of fact and interpretation are the sole responsibility of the author.

CHAPTER ONE

RIDING THE BELTWAY BUZZ:

What's all the fuss about a TV show?

On September 22, 1999, TV viewers across North America sat down to watch the pilot episode of a new primetime series on NBC.

There had already been a good deal of buzz about the new show, and advance notices had pointed out that its cast included veteran TV and movie performers such as Martin Sheen, Rob Lowe, Moira Kelly, Bradley Whitford, Allison Janney, and John Spencer. The presence of Sheen in particular caused something of a stir — the actor had already made his mark in a number of classic films such as *Apocalypse Now* and *Wall Street*, and had been very active politically throughout his career, but an actor like Martin Sheen signing on to do a weekly TV show was something to wonder about.

The show's promotional campaign made reference to some heavy hitters behind the cameras as well. The series — to be called *The West Wing*, a reference to the part of the real-life White House where the U.S. president and his staff go about the daily business of running the country — would be produced by Emmy-Award-winning veterans John Wells, the mastermind behind the long-running NBC mega-series ER, and Tommy Schlamme, who had directed numerous top-level TV shows, HBO comedy specials, and movies.

Most importantly, critics and fans alike noted that at the very heart of the new series was its creator, executive producer and writer Aaron Sorkin. The 38-year-old Sorkin had written the hit stage play *A Few Good Men*, and had added the screenplay to the 1992 movie version of it that starred Tom Cruise, Demi Moore, and Jack Nicholson. He'd also written the successful 1995 film *The American President* with Michael Douglas, Annette Bening, and Michael J. Fox, had co-written the 1993 thriller *Malice*, and was in the midst of writing another popular TV series airing on ABC at the time, *Sports Night*. Clearly, this was someone who knew how to develop intense, colorful characters for the screen, and, given his experience on *The American President*, how to research and write a script about how the U.S. political system worked on its highest levels.

From the outset, it had been clear that Sorkin harbored some pretty ambitious plans for the new show. In late July of 1999, two months before the pilot was to air, Sorkin, Wells, Schlamme and actors Rob Lowe, Richard Schiff, Martin Sheen, John Spencer, Bradley Whitford, and Allison Janney addressed a group of TV critics in Los Angeles for NBC's summer press tour. Most of the critics had seen the pilot episode, and were eager to ask the cast and creative team how they felt the new show would be received by TV viewers. As usual, the hyper-talkative Sorkin provided most of the answers to the critics' questions.

Many queries focused on just how big a role the American political system was going to have in the new series. "Obviously, politics is going to play a part in the show," Sorkin said. "But your enjoyment of the show really isn't going to depend upon whether you agree with that episode politically or whether you agree with [a] character politically. Issues are going to be on the show, but really only as fodder for drama. The show is probably going to be all over the map, populated with characters who are able to argue all sides of an issue."

Given all the advance promo, it wasn't all that surprising that the pilot episode scored well in the ratings. It achieved an overall audience of 16.9

million viewers — NBC's best debut series opener since 1994. From a critical perspective, what was even more surprising was the way the first episode unfolded on the screen.

The pilot's early scenes focused primarily on the President's staff — communications director Toby Zeigler (Schiff), chief of staff Leo McGarry (Spencer), press secretary C.J. Cregg (Janney), deputy chief of staff Josh Lyman (Whitford), and Deputy communications director Sam Seaborn (Lowe) — and viewers were given a quick introduction to the characters and their personal styles. Of particular interest was the development of the Sam Seaborn character through his unwitting liaison with Laurie, a Georgetown University law student who moonlights as a prostitute. As Laurie (played by Lisa Eldelstein) is smoking an early-morning joint after a night of passion with Sam, a mobile pager goes off, which she thinks is hers. She discovers it's not, and reads its message off to Sam: "Potus in a bicycle accident."

Of course Sam knows exactly what the message means — "Potus" is actually P.O.T.U.S. — an acronym used by real life White House staffers as shorthand for "President of the United Sates."

The news galvanizes Sam and he scrambles into his clothes. Apologizing, he rushes off, but not before Laurie, amused at the "Potus" message, tells him, "Your friend has a funny name" — to which Sam replies, "It's not his name. It's his job."

What's interesting about the pilot episode of *The West Wing* was the way the viewers were being manipulated. As the show unfolded, it appeared the focus was going to be on the White House staff and not the one person around whom everyone and everything else revolved — the President. From the opening sequence, it quickly became clear (or so it seemed) that the show — and the series — was going to be driven by a truly "ensemble" cast of solid and accomplished actors. And every one of them looked capable of carrying their scenes and characters so convincingly they deserved the "co-star" label.

All the speculation ended during the final minutes of the pilot episode with the dramatic appearance of Martin Sheen. Anyone watching quickly realized that if anyone in the cast was destined to earn star status in the series,

The West Wing gang from season one, including the show's creative team of John Wells and Tommy Schlamme (bottom row, second and third from right) and Aaron Sorkin (top row, third from right) PAUL SKIPPER/GLOBE PHOTOS

it was going to be him. TV critic Eric Kohanik recalls Sheen's entrance and impact — and what it meant for the show: "In the first episode, he was only in the last sequence, but his presence was so powerful," Kohanik recalls. "Sheen is not a big guy but you get this sense of power and charisma with him — it is a huge draw. When [the show's creative team] saw the impact he had in that first episode — once they saw him put the words into action — I think they had a vision in mind and when they saw him they changed it. He is a mesmerizing presence — he has such passion and charisma, it is easy to see why he has the effect that he does."

None of that diminished the importance or impact of the ensemble cast, but it was clear that Martin Sheen's Jed Bartlet was going to be a kind of first among equals on *The West Wing*. He wasn't just their boss — he was leader of the most powerful nation on earth. Even more important, his presence was clearly going to be huge in a series that many thought was going to have Rob Lowe as its main attraction.

During subsequent weeks, it also became apparent that *The West Wing* was growing into one of those classic TV shows whose impact went far beyond its weekly allotted hour. People started talking about it around the office water cooler and at parties. Each week, the various ethical dilemmas that had been raised and debated became fodder for real life discussions over coffee, in kitchens and bars, and in the pages of newspapers and magazines. Inevitably, in this age of electronic communication, many discussions were showing up on the growing number of fan-created Internet Web sites.

Was it wrong, for example, for deputy communications director Sam Seaborn to spend the night with a prostitute? How should chief of staff Leo McGarry deal with the staffer who leaked information to the press about her boss's alcoholism? What was going to happen with the inter-racial romance between President Bartlet's daughter Zoey and his personal assistant Charlie (played by Dulé Hill)? Would it be unethical for press secretary C.J. Cregg to begin a relationship with a reporter from the *Washington Post* (played by Timothy Busfield of *thirtysomething* fame)?

The show's popularity — during its first few months, it maintained a consistent audience of nearly 14 million viewers in the U.S. and an even higher per capita rating in Canada — and all the discussion surrounding it built to a fever pitch by the end of *The West Wing*'s first season. In a move strongly reminiscent of the 1979–80 *Dallas* season finale 20 years previously, Sorkin and his team concocted an episode that ended with wild shooting at a "town hall" meeting attended by all the regular West Wing staff. As the episode and the season ended, it was impossible to tell exactly who had been hit, which led to an entire summer of "who shot J.R."-like speculation.

It all formed a nice backdrop to the 2000 TV awards circuit. If any proof was needed that *The West Wing* had indeed put together one of the all-time greatest rookie seasons in TV history, the amount of hardware it took home during the off-season ended all speculation. At the annual Television Critics Association (TCA) awards in July, it became the first series in history to cop awards for drama of year, best new program of the year, and program of the year. And at the Emmy Awards ceremony in September, *The West Wing* made history, capturing a record nine Emmys, the most ever for a first year show and its cast.

Into its second season, the series just seemed to get better and better. The opening double-length episode, entitled "In the Shadow of Two Gunmen" drew a huge audience of nearly 25 million viewers, and was accompanied by a barrage of press in the days leading up to and immediately after it. As the season unfolded, the introduction of a number of new characters — and new plot lines — kept it at the forefront of the TV-viewing world, even with the appearance of a slew of new "reality" shows such as *Temptation Island* (which Fox aired in the same Wednesday night time slot) and *Survivor: The Australian Outback*.

But why do critics and watchers like *The West Wing* so much? What is it about the show that draws millions of viewers to it every week? Why do critics think the show "works" — and on what levels?

Why do increasing numbers of viewers take their fandom to extreme levels — far beyond most people who simply like the show enough to tune in every Wednesday night — by developing Web sites, writing "fanfic" (short stories with the show's characters in starring roles), and spending hours talking to other devotees in on-line chat rooms?

Does *The West Wing*'s success stem from its realistic portrayal of Washington politics, or from its presentation of an idealized president and bureaucracy — a kind of exercise in political wish-fulfillment? How do the show's producers bring the experiences of real-life people who have contributed their expertise to various presidential administrations into the production of the show? And what do people who make their living from observing the Washington political scene think about it — both as entertainment and as a mirror of the real thing?

Perhaps most importantly, how is the show put together? How did Aaron

Sorkin conceive it, how does he write it, and how is it crafted into a solid one-hour (actually about 45 minutes plus the commercials and credits) package every week? And how has it all played out on the small screen?

These are the questions that will be examined in the pages ahead. So, stay tuned, and get ready to enjoy an inside look at *The West Wing*, one of the smartest and most original TV series ever made.

CHAPTER TWO

WEST WING-ING IT

How the show moves from Aaron Sorkin's brain to the television screen

"There's a great tradition of storytelling that's thousands of
years old, telling stories about kings and their palaces,
and that's really what I wanted to do."
— Aaron Sorkin on PBS *NewsHour*

In the pilot episode of *The West Wing*, there's a gripping scene that introduces viewers to Martin Sheen in the character of President Josiah (Jed) Bartlet for the first time. Until now, you've only heard the other characters talking about him, and you've learned, at the very least, that he's not much of a cyclist. But in this scene, late in the episode, presidential staffers Josh and Toby are embroiled in a bitter argument with Christian fundamentalists Mary Marsh (played by Annie Corley) and the Rev. Al Caldwell (F. William Parker). They're feuding about Josh's appearance on TV trashing the religious right, making comments that have enraged Marsh and Caldwell. Suddenly, you hear a booming voice coming from off camera.

"I am the Lord your God. You shall worship no other God before me," the voice intones, and then puckishly adds, "Boy those were the days, huh?"

We discover the voice belongs to Bartlet, and although some may have thought he was referring to himself, it turns out that he's just using the biblical quote as a forceful way of involving himself in the argument. The president quickly breaks up the heated debate and sends the fundamentalists packing. The scene immediately paves the way for the Bartlet character for the rest of the series — he's a learned man with a sense of humor, a man of action, and, above all, someone with some very strong convictions.

The "Lord your God" scene makes for a captivating piece of drama and an excellent introduction to the show's main character, but it's also powerfully representative of how *The West Wing* is put together as a show. That's because — without going too overboard with the religious metaphor — *The West Wing* has its own "supreme being," and from whom all the episodes, characters, and energy flow. In the same way the pilot introduced Josiah Bartlet as the center of *The West Wing*'s on-screen universe, the show's real-life core is also embodied in one person — series creator, executive producer, and writer, Aaron Sorkin.

Of course, Sorkin has lots of help. Nobody, even someone as talented and driven as Sorkin, would be able to produce 22 weekly episodes of a high-quality show like *The West Wing* without a tremendous support team. Looking at the show's all-star cast and its experienced and accomplished staff of co-producers, directors, co-writers, and actors, it's clear that this team has talent and drive to spare.

Still, you can't ignore the fact that the acclaim that *The West Wing* has won over the past two seasons — from both the critics and the viewers — is a direct result of Sorkin's abilities. At the very least, he's written or co-written every one of the 44 episodes aired up to the end of the 2000–01 season. Also, the very idea for the series was Sorkin's brainchild. He's credited with being the *The West Wing*'s official creator — which in TV lingo, technically means nothing more than "writer of the pilot episode" — and in reality has made every single important creative decision regarding the show since its inception.

So who is Aaron Sorkin? Who is this person whose basic ideas about transforming the upper echelons of American politics into entertaining, fictionalized drama, somehow make it onto our TV screens for a well-acted hour every Wednesday night? Where does he get his ideas for the show, and how does he turn them into award-winning scripts? And what part does the rest of *The West Wing*'s production team play in the process?

First, the basics: Aaron Sorkin was born on June 9, 1960. The son of a lawyer father and a teacher mother, he grew up in Scarsdale, NY. Part of the Sorkin myth concerns two snippets from his childhood.

Apparently, he demonstrated an incredible knack for picking up dialogue as a kid. As he told Patrick Goldstein of the *Los Angeles Times*, instead of putting in long hours studying the Torah, he went to his rabbi and told him, "'I have a very good ear. Just speak [the Hebrew] into a tape recorder and I'll learn it.' It's my gift. I can give the impression of being a very bright, interesting person that you'd want to invite over for dinner."

The second Sorkin childhood anecdote (one that fans of *The West Wing* will no doubt interpret as foreshadowing his later career) was related in an in-depth profile in *George* magazine:

> At age 11, Sorkin volunteered to help out at George McGovern headquarters, mostly to impress a girl in his class. Incumbent Richard Nixon was on his way to White Plains, New York, for a rally, and the McGovern volunteers were deployed with signs that read, "McGovern for president". Just as Nixon's motorcade came around the bend, an old lady came up behind Sorkin, grabbed his sign, beaned him with it, and then stomped on it. Part of him, Sorkin says, has been trying to get back at that lady ever since.

Armed with these two childhood traits — a knack for dialogue and a passion for patriotism and liberal politics — it's not totally surprising that Sorkin would one day go on to write a show like *The West Wing*. But there were a number of stops along the way.

As a child, Sorkin loved to go to plays in Manhattan, often sneaking in after the first act. He later joked that he'd seen the second act of more plays than anyone else in the city. He later attended Syracuse University in upstate New York, majoring in musical theater. He began acting in children's theater in New York City, supporting himself by working as a theater bartender. Not making as much progress as he'd hoped as an actor, Sorkin began writing plays "out of an actor's frustration," a childhood friend told the *Times*. He started writing a play called *A Few Good Men* on cocktail napkins in between slinging drinks during show intermissions. Sorkin had heard about the real-life story involving a Navy lawyer upon which he based the play from his sister, who, coincidentally, is a Navy lawyer.

There must have been some magic in those napkins, because *A Few Good Men* was eventually produced on Broadway and ended up earning Sorkin the Outer Critics Circle award for Outstanding American Playwright in 1989. As an encore, Sorkin then wrote the off-Broadway comedy *Making Movies*.

He traveled to Los Angeles to work with director Rob Reiner on the film adaptation of *A Few Good Men* — he has the writer's credit on the 1992 film — and it was there that he had his first revelation about how the Hollywood power structure really works. In his first meeting with Reiner, also attended by a team of production executives, somebody made a critical comment about the story ("gave a note" in Hollywood argot) that sounded ridiculous to Reiner.

"Rob got up and said, 'There's too many goddamned people in this room,' and he threw everyone out but me," Sorkin told Goldstein:

> I realized what a difference it made that he was not
> only the director and the producer, but his company,
> Castle Rock, owned the movie. When you have these

party crashers who demand that you collaborate with them even when you never asked for their help, you have to tell them there's too many damn people in the room.

The screen version of *A Few Good Men* was nominated for four Oscars and five Golden Globe Awards, including best picture and best screenplay. After production wrapped up — and just before Jack Nicholson's famous high-voltage line, "You can't handle the truth!" became one of moviedom's most quoted phrases of the decade — Reiner commissioned Sorkin to write another screenplay that eventually became *The American President*. Originally, the script was a whopping 385 pages long, and Hollywood legend has it that Sorkin barricaded himself in the Four Seasons Hotel to write it, cranking out page after page after page in a marathon writing session and delivering the final draft to Reiner in a shopping bag.

The time Sorkin invested in writing *The American President* in his hotel room had four very important dividends for his career. First, it produced an impressive script about a widowed president (Michael Douglas), who falls for an attractive lobbyist (Annette Bening). It was made into a successful film that also starred Michael J. Fox, Richard Dreyfuss, and, coincidentally, Martin Sheen in the role of the president's close friend and advisor, A.J. McInerney.

Second, Sorkin's research efforts — which included trips to the White House to capture the look and feel of the place — gave him some valuable fodder for the pilot episode of a future series called *The West Wing*.

Thirdly, during those long nights writing the script, Sorkin kept the TV on for company, often tuned to the all-sports cable network, ESPN. He paid particular attention to ESPN's evening highlight-wrap-up show *SportsCenter*, then hosted by the dour Keith Olberman. The casual, well-informed banter among SportsCenter's talking heads formed the basis of another TV show he'd soon write — *Sports Night*, which aired on ABC from September 1998 to early 2000.

Finally, Sorkin's all-out burst to finish *The American President* had an

Aaron Sorkin, The West Wing*'s creative mastermind*

AP PHOTO/MARK J. TERRILL

unfortunate side-effect — he became a freebase cocaine addict. "I was the kind of addict who was functional," he told the *L.A. Times.* "I was actually writing good material. But I didn't see people or talk to people. I'd fax my pages over to Rob at 7 a.m. and after we'd talked about it, I'd close the curtains and start writing again."

Things did not get any better when *The American President* went into production, to the point where Reiner realized that he needed to do something to help the young writer who was clearly in trouble because of his coke dependence. Reiner asked one of his studio lawyers, Julia Bingham, to help Sorkin get into a rehab clinic. Bingham got Sorkin admitted to the Hazelden rehab center in Minnesota, where he spent the next 28 days kicking the cocaine habit.

Ironically — and perhaps fittingly for someone who makes his living writing drama — Sorkin's rehab experience had another positive outcome: he and Julia Bingham fell in love and married in 1996. There's a further irony in their marriage, as Sorkin explained to the *Times*: When his wife worked at Castle Rock, her job "was to see that I got as little money as possible," something he said he reminded his wife about repeatedly when they were house-hunting. Sorkin and Bingham now have a young daughter, but have recently separated.

Free of his cocaine problems but still possessed of tremendous energy and ambition, Sorkin ploughed on with his writing. He finished the pilot to the *Sports Night* series, which then sat on the desks of numerous TV execs for the better part of two years before Sorkin and Imagine Television producer Jonathan Krantz — son of the renowned romance novelist Judith Krantz — sold the concept to ABC.

Sorkin also enlisted the help of veteran Thomas Schlamme to direct, and the show built a solid cast that included Felicity Huffman (who has also appeared as a guest star on *The West Wing*) and Robert Guillaume.

While *Sports Night* got underway on ABC, Sorkin was also busy putting together the finishing touches on the pilot script for a new show about life among a team of presidential staffers. Most of the work he did on the new show's pilot came out of the ideas formed while he was writing *The American President.* "Since I had done it, I wanted to write more, somehow [about life in the White House]," recalled Sorkin, "and the stories that were coming to me were episodic. They seemed like chapters in a novel."

In order to pursue this new idea for a series, Sorkin's agent arranged a meeting with ace-producer Wells. "I wanted to meet him just because I was a fan. I thought, 'this will be a nice lunch to have,'" remembers Sorkin. "Almost as soon as I sat down, I realized that John Wells is an awfully busy guy. He's expecting me to pitch him something. . . . And so, on the spot, I started saying . . . 'What about the White House?' And that all happened quickly."

Soon, Wells became interested in producing the series, and the rest — at least from the standpoint of an ambitious writer hooking up with a veteran producer — is history. *The West Wing*, however, wasn't John Wells's first experience with an extremely successful TV show. He also produced the long-running and super successful NBC series, *ER*, and knew how to turn realistic situational drama into a rating winner. "Every three or four years, a show hits a pop sensibility," Wells told *George* magazine:

> People forget that *ER* came on in the middle of the
> Clinton health care debate. When we were on the cover
> of *Newsweek*, the headline was, 'A health care plan that
> really works.' That was what we tapped into. And
> that's what happened when *The West Wing* came on.
> We'd reached a point in the culture where we assumed
> that people who want to choose public service have
> the basest of motives of self-aggrandizement and
> financial gain.

Inside observers of the TV scene immediately sensed that there was something unusual about the Sorkin/Wells team-up. Wells had long been known as one of Hollywood's more meticulous producers, and it was no accident that he'd crafted *ER* into one of the best-rated series since its 1994 debut. It was also said he ran a tight ship on pretty strict deadlines — not exactly a conducive atmosphere to someone like Sorkin who had a habit of cranking out scripts at the last minute.

Of course, the critics assembled on the NBC Press tour in July 1999 were eager to know how the two would get along. "Well, I try to get him to be more like me," joked Wells, "and he tries to get me to be more like him."

Typically, Sorkin was a bit more effusive. "When we started, we had made the pilot and NBC let us know that we were on the fall schedule and it was time to get geared up," he recalled. "You know, John has an incredible machinery, a piece of apparatus. John Wells Productions is a very tight organization, and they issue a lot of pieces of paper. One of which give me a schedule for outlines and first drafts and second drafts, polished second drafts. And I read this and

I called John and said, 'John, have we met?' But so far it's working out fine."

For his part, Wells told *Newsweek* that their conflicting styles was no big deal. "Aaron likes to paint himself as a bad boy," Wells said, "but there's always a script, and it's always good."

Another thing confounding the critics was the fact that Sorkin, until ABC yanked *Sports Night* in February 2000, was writing scripts for two weekly series at the same time. TV critics asked him about it at a summer 1999 press conference, and Sorkin explained his schedule:

> In terms of 'It's going to be 60 percent here, 40 percent there,' I don't think it is going to be like that. I think that I'm going to be working on whatever is closest to my face at the moment. . . . The only thing that makes it even doable is that Tommy's doing it too. . . . How many episodes am I going to write? As many as I can. I love writing *The West Wing* . . . and if somebody comes along and offers you the opportunity to write this show, with this cast, with Tommy directing, with John producing, on this network, and [if] the downside of the deal is that you get to sleep a couple hours less every night, I think you take that deal and you run.

Getting by on a lot less sleep is one thing, but what about how your life actually pans out when you're trying to write high-level scripts for two prime-time shows every seven days? *Entertainment Weekly*'s Ken Tucker asked Sorkin about his writing schedule during a particular week early in 2000. "Ordinarily, I finish a *Sports Night* script by Sunday night, the cast reads it Monday morning, we rehearse Monday and Tuesday and we shoot Wednesday, Thursday and Friday," Sorkin explained. "I write *The West Wing* while they shoot *Sports Night*, but this time I didn't get *Wing* done in time."

And what happens if you're a victim of writer's block, right in the middle of a pressure-packed schedule like that? Just before the 2000–01 season began,

TV journalist Eric Kohanik asked Sorkin, "What is the tried and true source you go to if all else fails and you need an idea for a script — where do you go?" Sorkin's answer, after a long — and for him, seemingly eternal — pause, was revealing:

> It's a great question to ask and I'm really searching myself because I have been in that situation and I have thought "just do this" . . . but the truth is there are a couple of different answers. Sometimes I'll go to some kind of public place, a diner or a bus stop, anytime where I'm likely to be overhearing a conversation, and I'll listen to that conversation. . . . [G]enerally you are coming in in the middle of it, and sometimes, somebody will say something that will make you think, "I wonder what that was about, what was the beginning of *that* conversation?" . . . There is a line in *The American President* — we come into a Christmas party and one of the characters is talking to some guest at the party and he's saying, "Militant women are trying to destroy college football in this country!" I wrote an entire scene after that. It was something that I heard at a bus stop, and I thought "I don't want to hear any more — that is just a great first line of a scene!"

Sorkin also told Kohanik that he likes to go for a drive and listen to music when he's looking for story ideas. "I think to myself, 'Boy, I would love to use this song at the end of an episode," said Sorkin. "It would be great to fade out as this song plays — what could be happening where you'd want this? I'll work backwards this way."

That dynamic worked to near perfection in an episode entitled "Somebody's Going to Emergency, Somebody's Going to Jail", a title that pop music fans will recognize as a line from Don Henley's "In a New York Minute." In the episode, Sam is helping a friend of Donna's investigate the possibility of a presidential pardon for her grandfather, who was charged with spying in the 1940s. But Sam is also trying to deal with a conflict with his own father, and as the episode ends with Sam discovering the truth about the ex-spy and arriving at forgiveness for his father, the Henley tune kicks in with great dramatic effect.

On the subject of music, it's worth noting the accompaniment for *The West Wing* is arranged by W.G. Snuffy Walden, the composer who gained fame for his work on *thirtysomething*, and has also contributed scores to other series such as *Felicity, Once and Again, My So-Called Life,* and (of course) *Sports Night.* The original music for *The West Wing* pilot had been taken from the 1993 presidential Kevin Kline movie *Dave,* but Sorkin — a big fan of *thirtysomething* — called Walden to ask him to score his new show about DC politics.

Director Schlamme, in addition to sharing the burden of doing *Sports Night* and *The West Wing* episodes for a while, was also charged with establishing a convincing set for the Washington-based drama. He started with the movie set from *The American President,* and, with the help of designer John Huttman, who worked on *The West Wing's* pilot, began adapting it for TV. Schlamme and crew went to Washington and were allowed to look around the White House at night for an idea of how things might be set up for the small screen. Schlamme recalled how the process evolved:

> [B]etween all of us, we designed the sort of space that kind of combines a lot of elements of the [real-life] West Wing. For instance, a communications department, which is . . . down in the basement. We put it on the other floor so you get this sort of 'all on one space' [effect]. The Oval Office is the Oval Office. The reception area is the reception area. We changed the cabinet room because on a television show, we don't need two conference rooms, so we made up another room that felt more like the mansion, and we opened things up a

bit. But in truth, Dee Dee Myers, who's working with us, came in and said, 'Boy this seems more operational than the real one.' The bigger cheat that we did, which is what's so shocking, when you go to the West Wing, is how incredibly intimate the whole place is, and how people are on top of each other.

Schlamme's mention of Dee Dee Myers also brings up an important point about how Sorkin *et al* put *The West Wing* together. In order to give the show a realistic flavor, Sorkin signed on the former Clinton press secretary-turned-consultant. Myers kept Sorkin and crew informed about how things actually happen in the White House. For example, she advised the show's production team to forget about donuts, bagels, and coffee as props for morning meetings because it just doesn't happen in real life. Myers also gave *The West Wing*'s creative team advice on what a high-level intelligence briefing looks like.

During the 2000 presidential election, Sorkin — amidst much speculation that he would have to change the political tone of the show in the event of a Republican win — hired two more well-known political figures as consultants. This time, they were Republicans: former Reagan and Bush press secretary Marlin Fitzwater, and one-time Reagan speechwriter Peggy Noonan.

"They probably wanted a Republican viewpoint," said Fitzwater. Replied Sorkin, "They were hired not so much for their Republican-ness as much as for their wisdom." In addition to Myers, Fitzwater, and Noonan, Sorkin also enlisted Democratic consultant Patrick Caddell, and Lawrence O'Donnell, a political columnist and former aide to New York Senator Daniel Patrick Moynihan, to help him get the show's political-insider feel just right.

Once Sorkin, Wells, and Schlamme had been established as the show's creative team — assisted by the various Washington insiders who would help provide the show's authentic feel — all that was left was to assemble *The West Wing*'s core cast (for more on each cast member, see chapters five and six).

Leading up to the show's first season, the persistent rumor in TV circles

Tommy Schlamme, John Wells, Martin Sheen, and Allison Janney celebrate the show's success at the 2000 Emmy Awards AP PHOTO/REED SAXON

was that *The West Wing* was going to be a star vehicle for Rob Lowe, and that his character, Sam Seaborn, would end up being the main focus of the show's action. It didn't quite work out that way.

For his part, Martin Sheen said the reason he decided to do a TV series after relatively little prior exposure "was simple: Aaron Sorkin and John Wells." Sheen was also very familiar with political roles, having played Robert Kennedy in the 1974 film *The Missiles of October* and JFK in the Golden-Globe nominated TV miniseries *Kennedy*. Added to those was his supporting role in *The American President*.

Lowe's decision to join *The West Wing* was also one based largely on Sorkin's reputation as an ace wordsmith, along with a more personal reason. "It was really two things. One was, as I get older and my kids get older, taking them over to [a movie shot in a foreign setting like] Sri Lanka for 16 weeks is a little less romantic than it used to be. So I wanted to have, like, a real life," he told reporters before the show's debut. "And then when I read Aaron's script, it was — I have to tell you it was as good as any movie I've ever read, and certainly better than any television show I have ever read. And so it was just one of those happy matches."

When he was asked in the middle of the first season whether he resented his second-fiddle status behind Sheen, Lowe shrugged the whole thing off. "That's a tabloid thing," he told *Entertainment Weekly*'s Ken Tucker. "I am in [the show] as long as I am creatively happy."

When told of Lowe's comment, Sorkin revealed that Lowe's desire for creative contentment was something he had to take into consideration when writing for the strong ensemble cast. "I hope he stays creatively happy for a long time," said Sorkin. "I want people who want to work, who want to run with the ball. . . . Each of these actors could carry his or her own show, so it's a very glamorous problem to have — getting the ball to each of them every week."

Sheen and Lowe provided the high-profile actors the show needed to draw in the star-hungry viewers at home, but Sorkin and Wells still needed to complete *The West Wing*'s staff — and nobody was prepared for the outstanding group of lesser-known (but not for long) actors chosen to fill those roles.

One of them, Bradley Whitford, was a long-time movie and TV mainstay, but not yet a household name. If people recognized him at all, it was probably as Eric Gordon, the mean guy in the 1995 Adam Sandler movie, *Billy Madison*. But the Josh Lyman character became an instant hit for Whitford during the 1999–2000 season (about the same time as his wife Jane Kaczmarek enjoyed equal status playing the harried mom on the hit Fox series *Malcolm in the Middle*).

In May, 2001, *Esquire* magazine came up with the novel idea of having David Whitford, Bradley's journalist brother, write a piece about what it was like to be a top-ranked TV star's sibling. In it, David recounts a tale of how his brother got the part of Josh on *The West Wing*, and provides some insight on how the show's creative team of Sorkin, Wells, and Schlamme went about selecting their new cast.

Sorkin and Whitford had first started working together when the actor took over the lead role (the one eventually played by Tom Cruise in the movie version) as the prosecutor in *A Few Good Men*. The two kept in touch, and when Sorkin wrote the pilot to *Sports Night*, the first person he showed it to was Whitford, who he'd had in mind as one of the show's sports anchors. But Whitford, already involved with a short-lived series called *The Secret Lives of Men* (it lasted only six episodes on ABC) had to decline. Once again, Sorkin came calling, this time with the pilot episode of *The West Wing*, in which he wrote the Josh character for Whitford, and tried "to throw it in his strike zone."

Whitford prepped obsessively for his audition for the part of Josh, and delivered his lines in front of Sorkin, Schlamme, and John Levey, the Warner Brothers' casting director. After what he thought was an extremely successful first reading, Whitford was then asked to do it all over again, in front of Levey, Schlamme, and John Wells. This time, Whitford had to read his lines with Moira Kelly, who was slated to play Josh's ex-love interest in the early episodes. Unfortunately, the team of evaluators concluded there was no chemistry between Kelly and Whitford. Levey then informed Whitford's agent that he was not going to get the Josh part.

On the Friday before production was supposed to start, however, Whitford got a call — he had been picked for a part on *The West Wing* after all. But it wasn't as Josh, it was as Sam Seaborn. "I was just, 'Nooo, no, no,'" Whitford told his brother. "So I called Aaron . . . and I just said, 'Aaron, I just feel this very strongly. . . . This isn't about me wanting a job. This is the only time in my life I will play this card. I am this guy; I am not the other guy.'"

In the end, Lowe agreed to sign on for the part of Sam — getting what David Whitford says was "what he was asking for, including first billing and more money than any one else in the cast, except Martin Sheen" — and Whitford was in as Josh.

Bradley Whitford wasn't the only up-and-coming actor to make it big via the new series. While Sheen and Lowe brought some big-star cachet to *The*

West Wing, it was two lesser-known actors chosen for the roles of the staff's press secretary and communications director who walked away with Emmy Awards at the end of the show's first season. Allison Janney, who played C.J. Cregg, and Richard Schiff in the role Toby Zeigler, copped Best Supporting Actress and Best Supporting Actor prizes respectively. They weren't complete unknowns before the show's opening episode — but their *The West Wing* work vaulted them into the top rank of contemporary TV actors.

Janney — the daughter of an actress and a jazz musician who grew up in Dayton, Ohio (as did Sheen and Lowe), was better known as a film and theater actress. She played substantial but not starring parts in films like Stanley Tucci's *Big Night*, Ang Lee's *The Ice Storm*, the politically-inspired *Primary Colors*, and the multiple Oscar-winner *American Beauty*. On stage, she'd enjoyed success in the 1998 Broadway production of *A View From the Bridge* by Arthur Miller, being nominated for a Tony Award, and winning the Outer Critics Circle Award. Her attempts to make it on TV, though, were constantly hampered because casting directors seemed to think that the 6-foot actress was too tall for the small screen.

"Years ago, one casting agent told me that the only roles I could play were lesbians and aliens," she told *People* magazine toward the end of her Emmy Award-winning season. "When I said that Sigourney Weaver was tall, [the agent] replied, 'Well, she is drop-dead gorgeous.' I could feel the tears brimming in my eyes."

But Janney, who turned 40 during *The West Wing*'s first season, kept at it, and it was her role in 1998's *Primary Colors* that convinced Sorkin she'd be perfect in the role of the wise-cracking, sometimes-klutzy, but supremely competent C.J. "When Allison fell down the stairs in *Primary Colors*," recalled Sorkin, "she really captured my heart. There's nothing she's not great at."

Richard Schiff was also a veteran of the stage and screen, but in his case, acting came after a stint as an on- and off-Broadway director. Following a move to L.A., Schiff got parts in movies like *Seven*, *Malcolm X*, and Steven Spielberg's *Lost World*. In all, he's appeared in more than 40 movies, and achieved limited fame for his role as Barry Roth on the series *Relativity*. It was *The West Wing*, however, that launched Schiff's career — the hang-dog expression and sometimes-soft-spoken-sometimes-explosive role of Toby seems tailor-made for Schiff.

Sorkin and team cast yet another veteran of the stage, film, and TV wars in the role of Leo McGarry, the White House chief of staff and Bartlet's right-hand man. He was John Spencer, whom TV watchers recognize from his role as the irascible New York lawyer Tommy Mullany in the popular series *L.A. Law*. Spencer, who like Sheen is a recovering alcoholic and die-hard Democrat, brought a serious but lovable tone to his role as Leo, especially in a first-season episode where one of his staff leaks information about Leo's former addiction to Valium and alcohol. Although he fires the woman, Leo hires her back by show's end — showing the compassion he often demonstrates in a tough-love kind of way with the other high-ranking members of staff.

While Sorkin and *The West Wing*'s creative team were mostly on the mark when they were putting together the original cast, one performer who was originally billed as one of the stars never made it past the first season. Moira Kelly, who began the series in the role of Madeline (Mandy) Hampton, had previously appeared in a number of films before starring in the CBS drama series *To Have & To Hold*. It now appeared that her star turn in *The West Wing* was going to continue her streak.

But in strong ensemble casts like the one that emerged on *The West Wing*, it is often difficult to spread on-camera time around to everyone's satisfaction — and that might well have been the reason for Moira Kelly's departure after season one. Sorkin explained the situation diplomatically: "Moira is a terrific actress, but we just weren't the right thing for her," he said. Partway through 1999–2000, said Sorkin, "She expressed that she felt the same way, and as a result, story lines haven't been invested in that character, because we knew that at the end of the year, we'd be shaking hands and parting company."

Indeed, during the summer of speculation over who'd been shot at the end of *The West Wing*'s rookie season, many watchers, aware that Kelly would not be returning, concluded that her character would be revealed as the one who'd taken the bullet.

With the idea for the show in place, the creative team assembled, and the main cast ready to go to work, it was time for *The West Wing* to hit TV screens across North America.

CHAPTER THREE

THE PRESS CORPS:

Critical reaction to *The West Wing*

"I've been told by people who know what they're talking about that the NBC show *The West Wing* presents a highly idealized view of the workings of the White House. It rings of truthfulness, though. It may not be realistic, but it feels real, and it feels right — if this isn't what the White House is like, it's what it *should* be like."
— Nancy Franklin, *The New Yorker*, February 21, 2000

Since the series' inaugural episode aired on September 23, 1999, it's no exaggeration to say that, for the most part, critics have been in love with *The West Wing*. With a few notable, and, it must be said, entirely well-reasoned exceptions, the popular media — critics in magazines and newspapers, on the Internet, and on radio and TV — have praised the show enthusiastically.

In this chapter, we'll look at the critical acclaim the show has received, as well as some of the criticism, in an attempt to emphasize the hot buttons the show has pressed for people who make it their business to report on what's good in the world of TV.

Coverage of *The West Wing* in the media has taken several forms, and has ranged in tone and scope from the highbrow — features in magazines like *The New Yorker*, *The Atlantic Monthly*, and *George* — to the mass-market, including profiles in *People* and on *Entertainment Weekly*. In the show's first season, there were thousands of words written about Aaron Sorkin alone. Folks wanted to know where his ideas came from, how he'd conceived of the show, and how, for a time, he was able to write scripts for both *The West Wing* and *Sports Night* during the same season. People were also interested in learning about *The West Wing*'s cast, especially since many of the actors were not exactly household names before the show started to rake in awards.

With all this curiosity, the media was only too happy to deliver the goods. The effect on viewers was two-fold. First, this mass of information combined to create a viewing audience that was highly-informed about the show and how it was made, and was thus able to watch it with a more keenly-trained eye, sensitive to both the nuances in dialogue and production, and to the real-life political scenarios it portrayed.

And second, the vast amount of information available on the series — especially on the Internet — led to the creation of a whole new breed of *West Wing* superfan.

In general, the praise that critics have heaped on *The West Wing* has focused on a few key areas: the writing, the cast, the show's excellent "production values" — camera work, its fast-paced scenes, the realistic set — and in general, the series' "smart" tone. It was no surprise, then, when a survey revealed that *The West Wing* attracted more viewers in the 18 to 49 demographic earning more than $100,000 per year than any other network series.

I asked the Television Critics Association then-president, Eric Kohanik about these dynamics, and if the average fan is aware of some of the sophisticated work involved in the making of each episode. "It is a unique series in many ways," says Kohanik:

The dialogue on *The West Wing* is unlike anything else on television, and the camera work is unique. The busy-ness of it is different as well. There are some shows that try to emulate it but I think it is so captivating that from the moment you turn it on, you have to concentrate and pay attention. Otherwise you will miss things. It's an intelligent show — not one you can "veg out" in front of. I think it appeals to an audience who wants to watch TV to be entertained, but also to be challenged. Unlike a conventional sitcom or another standard type of drama, this one challenges you in a different kind of way: intellectually.

All that intelligence was not lost on the folks who give out the awards to TV shows during the summer off-season. At the TCA Awards held the summer after the series' rookie season, the show was recognized by critics as Drama of the Year, Best New Program of the Year and Program of the Year — the first time a show had captured all three prizes in a single season. And at the 52nd Annual Primetime Emmy Awards held on September 11, 2000, just before the show's second season was to begin, *The West Wing* (which had also received a record 18 nominations) copped nine Emmys — a record for a first-year series. It won the big one, Best Drama, over its much-touted rival, HBO's *The Sopranos*, as well as Best Supporting Awards for Richard Schiff and Allison Janney.

Martin Sheen at the 2000 TV Guide Awards

FITZROY BARRETT/GLOBE PHOTOS

Thomas Schlamme won for Best Directing for a Drama Series, and Sorkin and his associate Rick Cleveland scored Best Writing for a Drama Series for the "In Excelsis Deo" episode featuring the story of Toby's compassion for a homeless Korean War veteran (see the Episode guide page 124). (As this book was going to press in July 2001, *The West Wing* scored 18 more nominations for the 2001 Emmys. That news came just before Janney, Schiff, Whitford, and Spencer signed on to stay with the show through 2005, ending a contract dispute after Warner Brothers gave each a big pay raise.)

Much of the material written about *The West Wing* focuses on one central question: How "real" is the show? Since it's based on an actual physical location and group of people who really exist, as distinct from, say, *Friends* or *Baywatch*, it's only natural that many critics would fixate on this issue. Added to that, Sorkin's use of real-life consultants like Dee Dee Myers and Marlin Fitzwater, and his characters' habits of spouting bits of legislation and national-deficit figures at will, caused viewers to naturally try to make comparisons between *The West Wing*'s fictional White House and the real one.

In September 1999, no less an authority than the *Washington Post* asked one of their veteran writers, John Harris, to watch the pilot episode carefully, and then to write about it in terms of its resemblance to the real one. When asked over the phone about the piece he'd written, Harris admitted that since the pilot, he'd actually watched *The West Wing* very infrequently. But he did tune in to the initial airing of the series, and here's what he wrote about its "realistic" feeling:

> That, presumably, is intended to be part of the show's appeal, allowing its audience to ponder: Is this what it's really like? The answer: Kind of. Maybe. If you are willing to overlook a lot. Or so was the guarded verdict yesterday from a variety of White House officials and reporters who cover the place, many of whom tuned in to monitor *The West Wing* for verisimilitude. People looking for exaggerations or plain inventions found

many to pounce upon. Yet President Josiah Bartlet's earnest, stumbling, disaster du jour White House has a familiar feel to many.

What series creator Aaron Sorkin has managed to evoke — with a sting — is the Clinton White House of 1993 or 1994. Bartlet's staff is by turns appealingly ideal- istic and gratingly full of itself. Heartthrob deputy communications director Sam Seaborn, played by Rob Lowe, is at once cocksure and gnawed at by episodic revelations that he is totally winging it. . . .

When people began to make comparisons between the fictional Bartlet White House and the real one at 1600 Pennsylvania Avenue, it was also inevitable that people would begin to ask themselves, wistfully, whether the fiction was preferable to fact. Such comparisons were even more vivid in light of the U.S. presidential election on November 7, 2000.

In the *New York Times* on December 31, 2000 just after George W. Bush's win in the real presidential election, Laura Lippman wrote a tongue-in-cheek piece called "The Lovable Liberal Behind Bush's Victory" in which she suggested that *The West Wing*'s Bartlet actually bore serious responsibility for the Bush win and the Gore defeat. "*The West Wing* is wonderfully acted," wrote Lippman:

> [W]ell written and, contrary to what conservatives believe, more devastating to the Democrats than any right-wing conspiracy. For while *The West Wing* is reliably liberal on major issues, it makes a counter- productive pact with its almost 20 million viewers: Stay home, surrender to this fantasy of a Democratic presi- dent who never abandons his principles and skip the real thing. . . . The show's creator, Aaron Sorkin, has been praised for his uplifting world view. Yet what

could be more cynical than spoon-feeding this
Pollyanna presidency to disenfranchised liberals.

Lippman cites a number of examples to bolster her case, including the
main plot line of the "Shibboleth" episode that aired on November 22, 2000.
In that one, President Bartlet had to decide what to do with the boatload of
persecuted Chinese Christians who were seeking asylum. Bartlet's solution
was to ask the Governor of California to order the National Guard to conve-
niently look the other way while the Chinese slipped out of custody. "To go
where? And do what?" asked an incredulous Lippman. "That apparently falls
under Mr. Sorkin's Don't Ask, Don't Tell policy. When the hour is up, the
hour is up, allowing Bartlet to avoid real-life consequences for his Hardy Boy
policy solutions."

Lippman is not the only writer from a high-profile publication to have
criticized Sorkin *et al* for what they felt was *The West Wing's* unrealistic —
and potentially politically damaging — portrayal of U.S. politics. In the
venerable *Atlantic Monthly* magazine, critic Chris Lehman describes the show
like this:

> . . . it has an overt agenda so breathtaking in its sweep
> that "ambitious" barely begins to sum it up: *The West
> Wing* sets out, week after week, to restore public faith in
> the institutions of our government, to shore up the
> bulwarks of American patriotism, and to supply a
> vision of executive liberalism — at once principled and
> pragmatic; mandating both estimable political vision
> and serious personal sacrifice; plying an understanding
> of the nation's common good that is heroically heed-
> less of focus groups, opposition research, small-bore
> compromise, and re-election prospects — that exists
> nowhere else in our recent history. . . . [B]ut all this
> tight moral choreography comes up considerably short

of serving as a prescription for even a convincing imaginary liberal revival. In fact, sustained exposure to the logic of the show's plot conventions, the jittery policy patter of its characters, and (perhaps most of all) its sonorous faux nobility inspires a singular distrust. . . . These symbolic posturings [against the forces of right-wing culture] can only spring from the Administration's sense of itself as a missionary outpost in a hostile and benighted culture.

What's worse, says Lehman, is that Bartlet and his staff place an undue emphasis on "feelings," both of the presidential staff and of the nation at large — "[I]n the thickets of controversy that crop up in the Bartlet Administration, the strongest objection to a policy or a decision to overstep protocol is usually that it doesn't feel right" — and that approach just does not, and in real life cannot, ring true.

But the best critical angle on the series is the one that actually realizes that — surprise, surprise! — *The West Wing* is, after all, just a TV show. Sure, it's a TV show based heavily on reality — no one involved with the show has ever said it wasn't — but what you see every week are actors, going through their actions as dictated by a script. Any attempts to look at *The West Wing* as somehow either descriptive of, or prescriptive for, a real presidency, are merely an amusing exercise in drawing parallels. But *The West Wing* is not political reporting. It's a fictional TV show, and anyone who forgets that is in need of a reality check. Sure, it's easy to suspend your disbelief and say that Bartlet would make a better real-life president than Clinton or Gore or Bush, but most of us realize that won't happen. The near-realism of the show sometimes causes viewers to forget that, or at the very least indulge in some wishful thinking.

Indeed, Aaron Sorkin has said many, many times that what we're watching is a work of fiction. When *George* magazine writer Sharon Waxman asked him about the link between staffers on *The West Wing* and the people who had worked in Clinton's real-life administration in a November 2000 story, Sorkin responded emphatically. "Those connections are really nonsense," he said. "I'm a fiction writer. I make those people up."

As early as 1995, people were asking Sorkin the same kinds of questions when *The American President* was released. In an interview with *New York Screenwriter* magazine, Sorkin quoted an essay he'd read by David Mamet on the subject of character portrayal and reality:

> [Mamet] bemoaned the actor's habit of saying, "Well, this is a character who wouldn't eat this for breakfast — he would eat this for breakfast." He lets us know in no uncertain terms, and I couldn't agree with him more, that this is a character who would do nothing except what is contained on these pages right now. This is a character and not a person. This is a character in a story which is not the same as a person in life. Sitting there thinking about what he's going to have for breakfast in the morning, you better be able to tell me what it has to do with what they want and how hard it is to get it. It's intention and obstacle. The structure is how you're going to deal with that intention and obstacle. Everything comes from that. What does the character want? What's stopping them from getting it?

For director Tommy Schlamme, any realistic pretensions the show might have are simply part of doing good TV drama. In the same way as he tried to give *Sports Night* an ESPN-like feel to it, Schlamme tried to make *The West Wing* seem real, without getting hung up on the need to have the show mirror U.S. politics. "If you do a show about politics, people have to represent a certain political allegiance," he told Bernard Weinraub of the *New York Times*. "If you do a show about cops, they have to shoot a gun; or a show about doctors, they have to save lives. You've got to be specific here. If you play it safe, there's not a chance the show will be successful."

So, it's a good thing to keep in mind that, for all its alleged parallels to reality, there is still a degree of character/reality separation going on in the mind of its creator. When writer John Podhoretz bellowed in a March 1999 cover story in the conservative *Weekly Standard* that, "These characters aren't human beings. They're noble soldiers in a noble cause, and they have been washed clean of every impurity because of it," he was parroting a stance often taken by conservatives who disliked the show's political leanings. But Podhoretz missed the point — *The West Wing* remains nothing more than a TV show.

Podhoretz and his fellow ideologues aside, many of those closest to the show have not held back in commenting on real-life U.S. politics. One of the most vocal has been Martin Sheen, whose criticism of George W. Bush has been unwavering, ever since Dubya started making a serious run for the presidency. "I think he's a bully," Sheen told *George*'s Waxman. "I don't think he has any heart. That scares me. I've seen him. I've watched him — he's like a bad comic working the room. He's too angry. He talks too loud. He's acting compassionate — it's not real. It's not there. I think he's full of shit, frankly."

If any actor has earned the spurs to pontificate on political causes, it's Sheen. He's been arrested more than 60 times for participating in anti-nuclear and pro-environment protests, and he appeared in special promo spots after the 2001 season finale of *The West Wing* exhorting viewers to get behind a real-life bill that would boycott the sale of diamonds mined in African countries with oppressive regimes. Still, even Sheen realizes that as far as his credibility as an expert on presidential politics and campaigning goes, he's at best a well-qualified actor. "I'm not the president," he told *Entertainment Weekly* in early 2000. "I think the Republic is actually safer that I'm not in the [real] White House."

In November 2000 a television crew from the CTV network — which carries *The West Wing* in Canada — traveled to L.A. to visit the show's set. Pamela Wallin, the popular Canadian interviewer, sat down with key cast members in a two-part special, and opened up the program with an interview with Sheen. She asked Sheen about a recent *New York Times* poll that revealed 75 percent of Americans said that they would vote for Jed Bartlet for president,

JOHN BARRETT/ GLOBE PHOTOS

over real-life candidates George Bush and Al Gore. "What does that poll say about your role as President?" asked Wallin. "Hey — what does that say about our culture?" responded Sheen. "We live in fantasy!"

Another *West Wing* cast member who's been blurring the lines between reality and TV fiction is Bradley Whitford, a self-confessed "white-bread pinko liberal," who campaigned actively for Al Gore in the presidential race, and who also has little good to say about the current White House incumbent. Recalling that in one of his pre-presidential speeches, Bush told listeners that Jesus was the political philosopher who had influenced him most profoundly, Whitford told *George,* "You offer up Jesus Christ in a debate — and then you execute more people than the other governors combined? Do you really believe that Jesus who himself was killed because of the death penalty, would be pro-death penalty? I think Bush is a hypocrite, and I think he's proudly uninformed."

CTV's Wallin also asked Whitford how his personal politics affected his role on the show. "If you are going to do a relatively smart show about Washington now, you have to *be* something," said Whitford. "You can't *not* have a position in order to do that — you have to be a Republican or a Democrat. Also, I think there is something inherently heroic about being a progressive Democrat in a way that is not heroic about being a conservative Republican."

Wallin also asked John Spencer and Allison Janney about the reality aspects of the show, and Spencer agreed that it was a mistake to take the show too seriously as political commentary. "We are an entertainment, first and foremost," Spencer said, admitting that, if anything, his personal politics were a fair bit further left than Leo's are on the show. "This is a one-hour drama — our venue is the White House, but we are there to entertain. If a byproduct is political enlightenment and education — terrific!"

For her part, Janney said that unlike Sheen, Whitford, or Spencer, she's no political junkie. "There is nothing I know about politics at all. Nothing could be further from my experience," she told Wallin, adding that she does support the Democratic party, and that "most things that C.J. speaks out for, I have no trouble with."

One intersection of real life and TV drama spotted by eagle-eyed viewers came in the first season, when Josh was seen carrying around a copy of the recently-published book *The Corruption of American Politics* by veteran journalist Elizabeth Drew. "I think the staff [on the show] is a better bunch of people than you usually run into in Washington," Drew told *Entertainment Weekly*. "This President is certainly a nicer, more even-tempered one to his staff than I've seen in a long while."

In the on-line version of the above-mentioned Chris Lehman piece, *The Atlantic Monthly* commissioned a number of Washington insiders to comment on the show and its reality-value. One was Lowell Weiss, a former editor with the magazine and a presidential speechwriter from 1997 to 2000, as well as an Al Gore speechwriter. Weiss was asked if he recognized the Clinton West Wing in *The West Wing*. Weiss's answer was instructive, especially in its comparisons of the show to other recent reality-based entertainment efforts:

> As with ER, the characters on *The West Wing* are distil-
> lations — that is, they each do the work, and have the
> density of experience, of ten or more people . . . also the
> show's depictions of the President's interactions with
> his staff stray quite far from the mark. In reality, Oval
> Office briefings are rarely strolling repartee sessions.
> Clinton is as unstuffy and down-to-earth as Presidents

get, but we, the hired help, would never think to address the President of the United States in the casual, insouciant way you see on TV every Wednesday night . . . but the biggest difference between the two [West Wings — the real and the TV one] is simply this: *The West Wing* is a fairy tale. . . . [But] was *Top Gun* bad for the U.S. Armed Forces? Is *ER* bad for hospitals or emergency physicians? Is *Law & Order* bad for law and order? Heck, no. Sure, they're fairy tales. Sure they're less complicated and messy than real life. But they've managed to raise interest and boost morale in important institutions, and they've encouraged many young people to set their sights on pursuing.

Weiss also pointed out that Washington observers had been noticing several smilarities between real politicos and those on the show. He offered the following list:

Bill Clinton — Martin Sheen (Josiah Bartlet)
Hillary Clinton — Stockard Channing (Abigail Bartlet)
Chelsea Clinton — Elizabeth Moss (Zoey Bartlet)
George Stephanopoulos — Rob Lowe (Sam Seaborn)
Harold Ickes — Brad Whitford (Josh Lyman)
Dee Dee Myers — Allison Janney (C.J. Cregg)
Mandy Grunwald — Moira Kelly (Madeline Hampton)

Another Washington insider who commented on the veracity (or lack of it) displayed by *The West Wing* was Dick Morris, who, until his resignation in 1996, was Bill Clinton's chief political strategist. Morris had been lured from the Republican party by Clinton after the Democrats lost the 1994 Congressional election — in much the same way Bartlet had Leo McGarry hire lawyer Ainsley Hayes to help *The West Wing*'s Democrats out. It's worth noting that the decision to give Ainsley a basement office was based on another real-life event. In a memo from Dee Dee Myers to Sorkin, she recalled that David Gergen, a Reagan and Nixon political consultant who was hired by Clinton's staff, ended up getting the old White House barbershop as his office.

Evaluating the episode "And It's Surely to Their Credit" (which aired on November 1, 2000 — see episode guide, page 153) in the *National Post*, one of Canada's two national newspapers, Morris wrote that, "I know just how Ainsley Hayes feels," as a Republican who defected to the "dark side" of Democratic liberalism. He did have one objection to her treatment on the show, related specifically to the bunch of dead flowers and note saying "BITCH" that was left on her desk:

> In the real world, her fellow staffers would not have been so kind as to provide such an obvious warning. They would have been innocent and accepting to her face and then leaked to the press whatever damaging information about her they could find. . . . I don't know how long Emily Proctor will last in *The West Wing*. I guess it will depend on how long her contract runs and how well her boss's ratings hold up. Just like me.

One critic who did seem to grasp the important but elusive schism between reality and filmed drama was *New Yorker* magazine's long-time TV critic Nancy Franklin. In a February 21, 2000, review Franklin analyzed the show's pros and cons as a work of entertainment, looking at aspects such as dialogue and plot development. Franklin also took a stab at the whole "how real is it?" question:

> *The West Wing* deals with real issues, such as hate crimes and gun-control legislation, and also with issues of perception — which in politics are no less real. The general citizenry is not privy to the fine details of spin-

doctoring and damage control in the White House —
what we glimpse is probably the tip of the iceberg —
but *The West Wing* makes viewers feel as though they
had a ringside seat in the Oval Office.

Part of the critical buzz centered on the fact that *The West Wing* started off
— and continued steadily over its first two seasons — as a "smart" show that
appealed to an audience looking for more than a midweek hour-long veg-out
session. Given the rise of the so-called reality shows in 1999, beginning with
Survivor and continuing on with programs like *Temptation Island*, which the
Fox network aired in September 2000 in the same timeslot as *The West Wing*,
it was clear that many fans still appreciated a well-written, superbly acted
hour-long drama.

Another piece of sound criticism on *The West Wing* appeared in the May
1, 2000, issue of the on-line arts and entertainment magazine, *Salon*. Critic
Jonathan V. Last looked at the show to examine why, in his opinion, *The West
Wing* could only have been written about a liberal presidency. The subtitle of
the piece was, "Why liberals can make good drama and conservatives wind up
with *Red Dawn*."

Last focused on the May 1, 2000, annual White House Correspondents
Association dinner, at which reality and fiction actually did mesh — the
evening began with a video short written and filmed by Sorkin, featuring the
cast of *The West Wing* and the real-life White House press secretary Joe
Lockhart walking through the show's set. The show also received mention
during President Clinton's speech to the correspondents, and the cast was
honored at the traditional post-awards party. "In the course of one night,"
wrote Last, "*The West Wing* cemented itself as the most-talked-about television program in the nation's capital."

For fans of *The West Wing*, the real value in Last's piece lay in his attempt
to explain why the show is so well-loved in DC — and, by extension, the rest
of North America. Acknowledging that Aaron Sorkin had intentionally
populated his cast with people who appeared to look like real Clinton-

administration White House staffers, and who spent Wednesday nights making decisions that could never be made in real life, he concludes that:

> But if *The West Wing* is silly as a political diatribe, it's brilliant as television. The writing — and there is no one to credit but Sorkin — crackles with energy. The dialogue ricochets from character to character with intelligence and precision. The pacing is swift and sure. The cast is professional and believable. And the production values are the best on network television — from the elaborate, burnished sets to the dynamic yet smooth camerawork.

Another observer of the DC political scene was also on hand to describe the 2000 Correspondents Association event — what she called "the ultimate intersection of Hollywood and Washington." *Washington Post* reporter Jennifer Frey took particular glee in noting the number of *West Wing* cast members on hand for the event, and described the confusion of one Chinese actress who, never having seen the show, couldn't quite figure out who were the real Washington figures and who simply played their fictional counterparts on TV. "Timothy Busfield, who plays a journalist on the show, attempted, briefly, to explain the gap between the real White House and the fake one, then totally gave up," reported Frey. "'Look,' he said, 'I don't know anything I'm talking about. I don't even know any of these people I'm supposed to be meeting tonight.'"

Still, it's hard to ignore the *The West Wing*-as-mirror-to-real-life-politics discussion — if for no other reason than there's been so much of it. Despite all the criticism of the show as an idealized version of an American liberal utopia, there were many on the left side of the U.S. political spectrum who said that the show was not liberal enough. These critics — including some from the NAACP — cited the pilot episode's lack of non-white characters in position of authority, pointing out that all the main characters in the pilot

It's Emmy time for Toby and C.J. as Richard Schiff and Allison Janney collect their awards RON DAVIS/SHOOTING STAR

(Bartlet, Seaborn, McGarry, Lyman, Zeigler, and C.J.) were all white, something that would never happen in a truly liberal, Democratic White House. While Wells was quick to point out that his track record on *Third Watch* and ER demonstrated a decided lack of racial bias in selecting casts, Sorkin accepted the criticism. "I genuinely appreciate the tap on the shoulder from the NAACP," he told Yahlin Chang of *Newsweek*. "And they're quite right about being upset." Soon after, though, a number of strong minority characters began appearing, starting with Bartlet's personal physician Morris Tolliver (Ruben Santiago Hudson), his aide Charlie Young (played by Dulé Hill), and admiral Percy Fitzwallace (John Amos) in the second and third episodes and later on, National Security Adviser Nancy McNally (Anna Deavere Smith) and Judge Roberto Mendoza (Edward James Olmos).

Milwaukee-based writer Fred McKissack, commenting on *The West Wing* in the May 2000 issue of *The Progressive*, takes the not-liberal-enough critique a leftward step further. Honing in on the "A Proportional Response" episode of the first season, McKissack looks at Bartlet's monologue as he considers his choices of an answer to the Syrians, who have shot down a U.S. military transport plane — one that was carrying Morris Tolliver and his wife and kids.

After the Joint Chiefs of Staff advise him of possible responses to the plane's destruction, Bartlet retorts with one of his fire-and-brimstone speeches: "Let the word go forth, from this time and place, gentlemen — you kill an American, any American, we don't come back with a proportional response. We come back with total disaster."

"Geez," writes McKissack, "that sounds pretty Reaganesque to me." He notes that Bartlet's final answer is to bomb two ammunition dumps and the building housing the Syrian intelligence agency, and asks, rhetorically, "How freaking lefty is it to bomb the Syrians anyway? That's all we need: another Hollywood production demonizing an Arab nation."

Other observers of the show who delight in right-vs.-left characterizations of the politics it portrays have noted that Bartlet's decision not to commute the death sentence of a prisoner in episode 14 ("Take This Sabbath Day") is a prime example that the show is more than a weekly commercial for Liberal values. The episode was also a real stretch for Sheen as an actor, since he's committed to non-violence in his personal politics.

Sorkin cites this episode and one that aired two weeks later ("20 Hours in L.A.") as illustrations that his show is not a one-sided liberal diatribe. In the latter, guest star Bob Balaban plays Ted Marcus, a powerful Hollywood producer and potential Democratic party fund-raiser who's prepared to pump millions of dollars into Bartlet's campaign — if only the President will go on record with a strong position on gay rights. But Josh, who's in Los Angeles to oversee a huge, celebrity-studded fundraising party, has to tell Marcus that the president isn't prepared to do this.

"See, I would disagree that this is a liberal show," Sorkin told *Entertainment Weekly*'s Ken Tucker. "[Bartlet] is a Democrat, [but] we have seen him be very hawkish in response to a military act, and [he didn't] commute the sentence of the first federal prisoner executed since 1963. We know now that he is not particularly vocal about gay rights and is trying to avoid the issue of gays in the military."

Amid all of the attention being given to *The West Wing* so far, it's important to remember the absolutely crucial impact of creator/executive director

Sorkin on the show's success. As the writer or co-writer of every episode, Sorkin masterminds all the action and dictates the behavior of all the characters. Indeed, for a time after Sorkin's April 2001 drug-possession arrest the future of the show was somewhat unclear, based on the fact that if Sorkin went to prison on possession charges, no one was sure where the scripts would come from, especially given his near-legendary habit of submitting them just before filming. But Sorkin was not given jail time.

Another thing to keep in mind regarding the Sorkin/*The West Wing* dynamic is that this series is just the latest in a line — a long line, one hopes — of dramatic pieces he's created.

One TV critic who's in an excellent position to evaluate *The West Wing* in light of Sorkin's past career is *New Yorker* staff writer Tad Friend. In its September 28, 1998, issue, Friend's piece called "Laugh Riot" looked at how Sorkin, Schlamme, and the other principals involved with *Sports Night* struggled with ABC over a number of production issues. The most crucial of these was the inclusion of a laugh track — Sorkin and crew didn't want one; ABC executives did. Friend's article was an in-depth look at the entire process of getting the revolutionary comedy-drama about life at an ESPN-like all-sports TV network picked up by a major broadcaster. It contains loads of quotes from Sorkin about his approach to writing and his dramatic leanings. At one point, when discussing the radical nature of *Sports Night* in the context of his career, Sorkin told Friend:

> In film, my critics will tell you that nobody hugs the middle of the road tighter than I do, and I do feel comfortable there — you don't watch *A Few Good Men* and go, "Wow, this is different!" But, while in any other art form mixing comedy and drama is three thousand years old, in the half-hour TV show it's unheard of.

In a telephone interview, I asked Friend how he saw *The West Wing* fitting in with Sorkin's overall body of work. "The chief similarity between *Sports*

Night and *The West Wing*," he said,

> is the way the characters talk — they all have that same
> wised-up, bantering rhythm that is Sorkin's trademark.
> The biggest difference is that having an hour to write
> about politics and national affairs gives him a lot more
> room to work than having a half hour to write about
> sports. The other significant thing that people are
> finding out about Sorkin on *The West Wing* is that he is
> a very funny writer, not because he's setting up a lot of
> jokes, but when you look at Josh and Donna and Toby,
> there is this tremendous sense of character-based,
> deadpan humor there, and yet it's tinged with a kind of
> melancholy. I think it's what viewers identify with most.

Of course, nothing that has happened on *The West Wing* has drawn as much critical attention as the first-season-ending episode, "What Kind of Day Has It Been?" which aired on May 17, 2000, and, after a long summer — made even longer than it usually is in the TV world by NBC's coverage of the Summer Olympics from Australia — the two-hour opener of the 2000–01 season, "In the Shadow of Two Gunmen" which aired on October 4, 2000.

Not since *Dallas*'s who-shot-J.R. frenzy of speculation in the summer of 1980 was there as much buzz about a show's season premiere than there was surrounding *The West Wing* during the summer of 2000. Critics and fans alike tried to guess who'd taken the bullet fired from the crowd at the town hall meeting, and they were spurred on by NBC's teaser spots asking "Who's been hit?" (the question the walkie-talkie voice kept asking at the conclusion of the season finale).

Many critics, though, were less than impressed at the way Sorkin and crew chose to end the series' rookie season. The memory of the *Dallas* summer of speculation was not all that far removed from many people's minds, and many pundits resented the melodramatic shooting followed by the "let's-wait-all-summer-to-see-who-took-the-bullet" wait as a cheap trick designed to boost ratings.

Even Sorkin was mindful of a possible descent into cheeziness by ending things that way. "I understand people's misgivings," he told reporters just before the second season's two-hour premiere went to air. "The cliff-hanger-ness of it all perhaps seemed a step down. Perhaps."

While the cliffhanger approach might have been seen by TV critics as an obvious attempt to bolster ratings, the viewing public did not seem to mind. Perhaps it was the Olympics-delayed start to the season, or maybe all the pre-election hype was getting people all fired up about politics. Maybe the cliffhanger finale did the trick, or maybe it was the attention drawn to the show by its nine-Emmy record performance the previous month. Whatever it was, people tuned in to the two-hour second-season opener in huge numbers.

The October 4 episode drew a whopping 25 million viewers in the U.S., and 2.2 million in Canada (the two figures represent roughly equal amounts in terms of per-capita watchers, since Canada has about one-tenth the population of its neighbor to the south). That figure was a pretty good start to the new season, too, since in the show's first go-round it had averaged about 14 million viewers per episode — good enough for 30th spot overall among all network series.

As presaged by the solid two-hour opener, *The West Wing* kept up its momentum going into its second season. Dramatically, there were several episodes that both critics and fans took to.

One of them was "Noël," scheduled to air on December 13, 2000. In a weird instance of life imitating art, the episode was pre-empted by a Gore/Bush debate and instead aired a week later. Even stranger was the fact that the show's Canadian viewers got to see the world's favorite show on American politics a week before their American counterparts, since the CTV network aired the episode in its original timeslot. The show answered several long-standing questions about Josh's state of mind following the assassination attempt, and guest-starred (another life-art intersection) cellist Yo-Yo Ma, as himself.

Another popular episode was "The Stackhouse Filibuster." In this one, the

78-year-old Senator George Stackhouse puts a wrench in everyone's weekend plans by launching into a long, nonsense-filled speech — mostly he reads recipes from an old cookbook — forcing a delay in the Senate. Hours later, Donna discovers why he's doing it (see page 171), and the staff figures out a way that he can be stopped without costing him his dignity.

This episode was important in assessing the whole reality-vs.-fiction debate on *The West Wing* because it required a working knowledge of U.S. politics if one wanted to evaluate it as an actual piece of real-life action. Although a good percentage of the show's viewership in the U.S. has a basic idea that something called a "filibuster" can be invoked as a delaying tactic, it's unlikely many Americans (and far fewer Canadians) know how it is used — and how it can be stopped. We had to trust that what the characters were telling us was the truth if we wanted to watch the show as a reality-based one. If on the other hand you didn't feel you needed the actual events to be true — if it was enough for you that they *seemed* realistic — then you could sit back and be entertained without such worries.

Another second-season show that resounded in the minds of many critics was the April 4, 2001 episode, "17 People." In it, Toby finally learns about President Bartlet's multiple sclerosis, leading to a bitter exchange with the President over Toby's right to have been told sooner, and more ominously, the possibility that the Administration may have perpetrated fraud on the American public by not disclosing the President's condition sooner.

One unabashed fan, the Canadian TV columnist Scott Feschuk, wrote that although "the show has worried me a bit of late . . . Wednesday's show, with its rancor and its absence of resolution, shifts *The West Wing* to more complex dramatic terrain, and augurs well for the final few new shows of the current broadcast year. Beyond that, the episode also stands, to these eyes at least, as the creative and acting pinnacle of the season."

Of course, what Feschuk was referring to when he spoke of "the final few new shows of the season" was the concluding quartet of episodes that centered on Bartlet's medical condition, his impending disclosure of it to the nation, and the will-he-won't-he-run-again decision about his possible second term as president. NBC publicized the episodes' guest star, Oliver Platt (in the role of Oliver Babish, the White House Counsel) in a number of dramatic spots, and it was clear that things were building up to another season-ending blockbuster with the final episode on May 16.

But the show-related headlines weren't all devoted to the fictional President's health in the weeks leading up to the 2000–01 season finale. Instead, they centered around Aaron Sorkin's real-life arrest on April 15 at the Burbank airport. Initially, news reports said that Sorkin was arrested for possessing illegal hallucinogenic mushrooms, found after an X-ray had indicated an unusual-looking package in his luggage as he prepared to board a flight to Las Vegas. Sorkin was released a few hours later after posting a $10,000 bail.

Two weeks after the initial arrest, Sorkin was back in court, pleading not guilty to two felony counts of drug possession — one for the mushrooms, and the other for a small amount of base cocaine that was also found in his luggage. Sorkin awaited a June 4 hearing in Burbank Superior Court, to decide if he was eligible for a drug rehab program. The *Los Angeles Times* quoted Burbank D.A. spokesperson Sandi Gibbons as saying that Sorkin's chances for a drug treatment program were "good because he appeared not to have any prior drug-related convictions." But, of course, he did have a long-standing bout with cocaine addiction — thought by most to have been kicked — in his past. In 1999, Sorkin had told the *Times* that "I'm the same as any other addict. I'm just a phone call away from getting loaded again."

Sorkin ultimately avoided going to jail, and was ordered instead to undergo rehab. But Sorkin's drug bust also must have put a strain on his marriage, as he and wife Julia Bingham were widely reported to have separated in late June 2001.

The very fact that Sorkin's arrest took much of the TV world's attention away from the season-ending series of episodes spoke volumes about *The West Wing*'s popularity. Just before Sorkin was busted, actor Robert Downey Jr. also made headlines for *his* arrest, the latest in an unfortunately long line of drug-related problems for the star of movies like *Chaplin* and *Wonder Boys*, and, more recently, the hit Fox TV series *Ally McBeal*. Downey's latest arrest led to him being booted off the show by creator/producer David E. Kelley, and the entertainment-page and tabloid coverage of Downey's descent seemed perfectly natural — after all, Hollywood-watchers love stories, happy or sad, about the faces they see in front of the camera.

But Aaron Sorkin is a TV writer — not some high-profile actor. When was the last time the travails of somebody who writes scripts for a living made headlines? It's a good bet the majority of even serious TV viewers barely know the names of the writers of their favorite shows, let alone details of personal lives. The fact that Sorkin's drug arrest made headlines at all was a vivid demonstration of how popular *The West Wing* — and its personalities — had become.

Shooting for the final episodes had already ended when Sorkin's troubles hit the headlines, and reaction to the second-season finale was mixed. Many felt that some of its dramatic devices were over obvious, and that the flashback scenes between Bartlet and his long-time secretary Mrs. Landingham (who'd been killed in a car crash in the previous episode) were contrived and gave away the ending.

The *Post*'s Scott Feschuk's review summed it up best. Feschuk spent the better part of his May 18 review trashing the episode and its mastermind: "Having watched the season finale of *The West Wing*, I can't say that it's surprising that creator Aaron Sorkin was recently busted at airport security for possession of hallucinogenic mushrooms," Feschuk wrote. "What is startling, however, is that he actually had any mushrooms left to haul around after writing that episode."

Still, though, Feschuk admits he wanted to have it both ways — to criticize the finale, and to praise it:

> I'm going to forget the bulk of this episode and instead
> remember its two sublime aspects: the fact that Sorkin
> resisted the temptation to manufacture cheap drama
> by exploiting the standoff at the U.S. embassy in Haiti,
> and instead focused on explaining the origins of the

relationship between Bartlet and his secretary; and, better still, the episode's concluding five minutes, almost all of which transpired without dialogue as the President traveled to the news conference which would come to define his administration.

In the end, the 2000–01 season finale was all that we'd come to expect from *The West Wing* — lots of good drama, great dialogue, and superb acting. A little over the top in places perhaps — and maybe even a little sappy. Without resorting to the first season finale's cliffhanger ending, Sorkin managed to end the show's second year with a great deal of panache.

CHAPTER FOUR

THE WEB WING:

Encounters with
the super-fans

"I really kind of live in fear of any *West Wing* Web sites."
— Bradley Whitford (Josh Lyman), as quoted on the home page of
the "Inside the Bartlet White House" site, at http://jedbartlet.com/

It's impossible to talk about *The West Wing* and the impact it has had on the larger TV viewing audience without talking about the show's presence on the Internet.

Actually, you could say the same thing about any popular series that made its debut during the last decade. Pick any primetime show from the '90s, and you'll probably encounter a raft of sites on the Net just by keying in the show's title. These sites come in two basic flavors — the official ones put up by the networks and/or studios, and the unofficial (and sometimes amateurish) sites developed by the die-hard fans. Official sites usually contain short cast and production team bios and pictures, brief plot summaries, occasionally a chat room, and often a link to other related sites. Just for the record, the official NBC show site is at **www.nbc.com/westwing**.

It's the unofficial sites, though, that hold the real key to what the viewers at home like about a particular show. These cyber-tributes are, after all, the work of dedicated — and sometimes obsessed — fans who have constructed an electronic testament to their love of a series, almost always for no monetary gain. These sites usually feature comprehensive bios of the stars, photo galleries (often containing pictures reproduced without permission of the copyright holder), an archive of published material on the show/cast (again, often reproduced without authorization), several forums for chatting or posting messages, extensive episode and "continuity" guides, and criticism/ reviews of individual installments. The unofficial sites also often provide an opportunity for cognoscenti to post "fanfic" — fictional works by fans in which a show's characters are featured in all manner of hypothetical plots.

The West Wing's presence on the Internet is a little different — especially when it comes to the non-official sites devoted to the show. Part of this is due to the nature of the series itself. One would expect fans of a "smart," witty show based on American politics would have lots to say, and in an interesting and entertaining manner. While there is an element of the "gosh-isn't-he/ she-cute and let's-speculate-if-character-X-and-character-Y-are-going-to- have-their-first-love-scene-in-episode-Z" stuff that pervades the fan sites of shows like *Friends* and *Dawson's Creek*, *The West Wing*'s unofficial sites tend to carry a lot more political and social freight and debate than the other sites.

In an attempt to get some insight into what drives the sites visited and maintained by these superfans, I contacted the owners of four prominent, unofficial *West Wing* sites. I asked them a series of almost-identical questions about *The West Wing*'s presence in cyberspace, their own specific sites, the kind of people who visit them, and what they feel are the reasons for the show's popularity.

I reckoned that these four people would probably know the show — and its fans — better than anyone else. I also figured that four people who were so into *The West Wing* they were prepared to spend a good deal of their free time building Web sites devoted to the show, simply for the sheer enjoyment of it, would have lots of interesting things to say. The people you are about to meet are not casual viewers of *The West Wing* — they are among its most dedicated and knowledgeable fans.

The quartet of *West Wing* web denizens include B.E. Warne, who masterminds the **westwing.bewarne.com** site; Susannah Nix, creator of **www.jedbartlet.com**; Lesley Gayle, the host of **www.testytoads.com/TWW**; and Rachel Vagts, who masterminds **thewestwing.tktv.net**. In keeping with the spirit of the Net and the technology that supports it, all the interviews were conducted via e-mail.

I began with Warne because I'd been impressed with the episode summaries I'd read on her site. She also appeared to be seriously committed to the idea of "continuity" on *The West Wing* (i.e., making sure the characters and events are presented consistently and logically in each episode). For those unfamiliar with the concept at its most basic level, here's an example of continuity gone awry. Suppose Josh tells C.J. in an early episode that he absolutely can't stand apples, and then in a later episode, he appears in a scene munching happily on a Granny Smith. Even if the latter scene lasts only a few seconds, it can drive continuity freaks batty. Some extra-long-running shows like the U.K.'s *Coronation Street* (40 years and counting), employs staff devoted entirely to keeping up each character's "biography" so that inconsistencies don't occur and the ire of watchful fans is not raised.

B.E. Warne, who lives in Albuquerque, New Mexico, started watching *The West Wing* with its pilot episode but had no interest beyond simply liking it. She says, for example, that if she was out on the occasional Wednesday night, she wouldn't bother taping the episode she'd missed. But that changed with the January 26, 2000 episode, entitled "Take out the Trash Day" — in which Leo confronts the staffer who leaked information about his alcohol/painkiller addiction (see page 130).

Warne describes how that one on-screen confrontation got her hooked:

The scene was extraordinary even in a show that often had compelling scenes. The following week *The West Wing* wasn't shown and I found I missed it. So I started calling everyone I know around the country to find people who either had tapes of past shows or who might know someone with tapes. Tapes started coming in the next weeks and I started watching them more closely than I had before.

Shortly after that, an arm injury provided Warne with more time than usual to watch the tapes that were coming in. Since her writing arm was uninjured, she was able to take notes while she watched.

When she started typing up the notes, she did them in HTML ("I actually think in HTML when typing"). Warne had previously completed an episode guide for the U.K. show *Blake's 7* for an American science-fiction magazine, and had also compiled a collection of quotes from the 1970s TV show *Kung Fu* that had appeared on computer bulletin boards in the pre-Web days and was later converted to HTML for the Internet.

With all those notes about *The West Wing* in place and in electronic form, Warne decided to put the material onto the Internet. She describes how it happened:

> Once I had the information down, I needed some kind of organization and navigation and so had to do some design work even though I am not a designer. Then I needed to put the Web site up and I went to my bosses and asked if I could put it up on our Web server (we design, maintain, promote and host Web sites). They agreed. At this point it is late June [2000].

All of this begs the question, *why* would anyone want to create a Web site devoted to a TV show? Warne responded:

I didn't set out to do a "West Wing" Web site. When I
did decide to put up my notes, it was aimed at Sorkin,
who I thought needed a resource for the information
that had already been established on the show. I don't
know why I collect quotations but I have been doing so
for more than two decades. I have hundreds of note-
books throughout the house of things I have written
down because I thought they were beautifully written,
profound, or strange and different in some way or
another.... Words that seem to reveal something about
the world that I thought might be true. Sentences that
revealed something unusual about a character. I rarely
read a book without having a notebook next to me. I
don't always do anything with notes, mind you, but I
take them....

It's rumored among fans of *The West Wing* that the plot and character
minutiae are stored in Aaron Sorkin's head. Warne calls this the show's
"Bible," and says that with *The West Wing*, she now had the opportunity to do
a continuity Web site for a show that was still running in prime time: "Here,
with *West Wing*... was a chance to actually create something that would help
those who were creating the show."

To that end, Warne wrote a letter to Sorkin after the site was up and
running at *The West Wing*'s production company (John Wells Productions).
She did not get a reply, and discovered that other fans she'd been in contact
with were having the same problem:

That's one of the purposes my site started serving.
Because people are not able to reach the show, they
complain to me and the site has expanded in directions
I didn't envision when I started the site. All because no

one connected with this show will respond to anything the viewers say. I had envisioned a site that would keep track of continuity and point out when the show contradicted itself. But Sorkin has been remarkably good at keeping track of what he has already said. But in not listening to the viewers, he actually did allow me a way of helping. I'm not helping the show itself but I do allow general viewers a forum in which to complain about factual mistakes and when they can prove to me that something is wrong, I put up their names with the information.

A big difference between Warne's site and the others is that hers provides almost no biographical information on the show's cast. "It isn't that I think this show would be just as good with other actors — actually, I think this set of actors adds tremendously to the show," she says. "But my site is about the world that Sorkin (and his actors, etc.) creates. . . . [T]here are other sites devoted to the actors and a person has to draw the line some place. And I find that the people visiting my site are not there to find out about actors."

In her work on her site, Warne has made a few important conclusions about the nature of *West Wing* fandom, and about the different varieties of TV show watchers in general:

> The term "fan" used to be a general term that encompassed all the people who liked a show or a movie. But then starting with *Star Trek*, people started to notice that there were people connected with certain shows who did more than just like a show. They attended conventions, wrote stories, published fanzines, wrote and recorded songs, corresponded with others who were obsessed with the show, and when video tape came out they exchanged tapes — some even made

original productions and sent those out to others. With
the advent of the Internet, people "gathered" first in
AOL (CompuServe, Prodigy, Genie) chats as well as
newsgroups (within those organizations and outside)
and computer bulletin boards to talk about the topic
they were fairly obsessed with. Later the Internet,
allowed them real-time chats with more and more
people — they could communicate not only with the
people inside the connecting service they belonged to
but outside of it with people not in AOL, etc. and with
people in the other competing services. There needed
to be a word that described such people. They became
known as the fans (for fanatics).

What about people who like to watch a given show every week, maybe
discuss it at work or with friends over a pint, and perhaps read about it in the
paper or a magazine, but don't take it beyond that? For them, chat groups and
Web sites — beyond a casual glance — just don't form part of the equation.
If they don't catch the show, they might tape it, but if they don't, it's no big
deal. These TV-watchers are likely the most common type of *The West Wing*
viewers — but what do you call them?

From personal experience, Warne has her own ideas about that group,
too:

I call them the faithful viewers. . . . [S]ometimes those
people missed a show or didn't remember a fact and
they did read articles on the show in magazines and
likewise if they were online they might check out
general Web sites to see if there was some information
on the show they might find interesting. Such people, if
they wanted to express themselves, might also occasionally want to write a letter to the show — general viewers

as well as fans might feel strongly about something on a show. Especially a show about politics about which many people feel strongly — probably a higher proportion of the people watching this show than the people watching most other primetime shows feel strongly about politics. So, even though they are not obsessed with the show (not up there with the people who devote huge amounts of time and energy to their feelings about the show), they may want to say something occasionally about something the show addresses. . .

Whether or not she's aiming her site at die-hard fans or faithful viewers, Warne has put it up with the main purpose of tracking the details of *The West Wing*, and allowing anyone with a similar attention to the finer points to have their say. Because *The West Wing* is a show that makes — mostly though Sorkin's efforts in writing and researching the scripts — a serious attempt to appear grounded in reality, each episode contains references to things that exist, or appear to exist in real life. Points of legislation, economic statistics, military equipment and strategy, and, given President Bartlet's religious bent, Biblical quotes, are the most common real-life points of reference. Being sticklers for details, Warne and her devotees have noticed lots of times when information on the show isn't quite right. She calls these "world differences," and describes them as "problems connecting the world inside the show to the world outside the show."

Warne says that spotting world differences is particularly popular with lawyers, people connected with the military, and (not surprisingly), Republicans and others at odds with Sorkin's positions:

> Such people are up in arms about anything that is contrary to fact that is connected with things they feel strongly about, such as their profession or their interests. . . . I understand the other Web sites about the

*www.jedbartlet.com
webmaster
Susannah Nix
with
Bradley Whitford
on Nix's visit
to the set*

COURTESY
SUSANNAH NIX

show don't get lawyers writing about what piece of law was discussed in a way that didn't make sense. They don't have fighter pilots writing to tell them that the plane that had been discussed in the previous episode couldn't do what the show said it did and that a particular general wouldn't have been a three star but would have been a four star general! These are the people who write me. . . . I make these people give me supporting information and I check it out and then put it on the site giving them a place to vent their frustration. I, personally, don't know the law well enough to even catch many of these mistakes (likewise I can just barely tell the difference between a 747 and an F-16).

Warne says that many of the incorrect facts on the show could be easily verified. She cites examples like Toby calling "Honor thy Father" the third

Janney and Nix are all grins during web-meister Nix's set visit

COURTESY SUSANNAH NIX

commandment, the continual references to military equipment ("The military personnel who watch are hurt by this and it reinforces the idea that liberals don't care about the military," says Warne), and Toby's correcting C.J. on the dates of events in early U.S. history, as just three examples of inaccurate facts that have appeared on *The West Wing*. Readers can check her site to find these and more.

All of this insistence on detail begs a couple of important questions. First, for most people who watch *The West Wing*, achieving a high degree of accuracy in relating real-life things to events on the show is not of crucial importance in their enjoyment of it.

Although various writers have called the show "educational" because of its insights into the inner workings of American government, nobody should ever suggest that *The West Wing* is a legitimate substitute for learning about civics and politics. It is, as Aaron Sorkin and others connected with the show have pointed out many times, a *fictional* depiction of life in Washington. It's a television show, after all!

There is the issue of wish-fulfillment, though. While people realize the events depicted on *The West Wing* aren't real, many wish that they were, or at least that real Washington politics would work that way. Here's Warne's take on this:

> I think most people wish that reality was more like the show. Clinton's moral lapses hurt us and it was nice to turn from that to see a president without such streaks of insanity. And now Bush is standing up saying that

the U.S. cares more about its current economic health than the future climate of the world and the climate changes already taking lives in the rest of the world. . . . I, at least, am ready for a vision of a President who doesn't embarrass me and shame the country! Bartlet & company are human enough to be semi-realistic but are also people we can respect. They are smarter than the guy currently in the White House. . . . To escape for an hour here and there, I turn to Bartlet. . . . Note, though, that I try to keep my politics out of my site. . . . There were *West Wing* sites which took sides in the recent Presidential election. I'm upset enough now, that I wonder if I did that right [keeping the site politically neutral] but I don't believe the site is a pulpit for preaching my views (though occasionally, if the show pushes me, I will make an editorial comment). . . .

With Warne's comments in mind, it is worth pointing out that there is a site called "The Left Wing" at **www.geocities.com/the_left_wing/main.html** — operated by a fan whose political views are the polar opposite of Sorkin's.

As the host of a Web site devoted to the show, Warne is in a prime position to assess exactly why *The West Wing* is so popular among fanatics, faithful viewers, and casual watchers alike. According to her, the answer is obvious. "The writing, of course," she says.

Sorkin's writing is spectacular and we, as TV viewers, are so pleased to see that level of writing devoted to television! And I think people also like to see something that makes them think (I could be wrong about that, maybe it's just the viewers I hear from). The acting is really extraordinary but it is the writing that give these actors something to do. The writing, the writing, the writing!

I also corresponded with Lesley Gayle, a woman in New York City (the name given here is a pseudonym) who runs the "West Wing Online" fan site at **www.testytoads.com/TWW**. It features a message board, episode transcripts, photos, and articles that have appeared in the press. There are also mini-movies available for downloading.

I began by asking her for a bit of history about the site — and about her decision to put it up. She told me that she compiled the raw material for the site in December of 1999, during the first few months of the show's inaugural season. She uploaded and opened it to the public the following January. Since she travels frequently, Gayle takes her laptop along to maintain the site. Exactly why she runs the site "is a little tougher to answer," says Gayle:

> I chose *The West Wing* because I really loved the show, and thought others probably did as well. Also, there was hardly anything out and about regarding the show, so at the time, my site was one of the few on the web, and one of the more comprehensive ones.

Gayle is in complete agreement with B.E. Warne about why *The West Wing* is so popular. "First and foremost, I think it's the writing," she says. "Second to that is the outstanding cast of actors, and finally, I think it's the topic. Politics are always of interest, so it's an attractive subject to a wide variety of people. But ultimately, it's going to come back to the writing."

What is Gayle's take on the *The West Wing*-as-reality issue?

> I think it's absolutely a fantasy president. This is the guy we'd like to see running the country, but in actuality? It would never happen! I'm not sure of course, but I doubt that such an honest and truly caring person would make it that far in politics. It seems to be a very dog-eat-dog world, and to make it all the way to

the oval office, well . . . it's not easy, and unfortunately I don't think too many sincere folks last in political life. There is realistic basis in the show from the standpoint that research on the issues is tasked; I think most of the facts and stats are correct. However, a person motivated so purely of heart, that's the fantasy. Week after week Bartlet comes into our living rooms, wanting to do what's best for everyone. He takes the little guy into consideration. I just don't think that's reality, which is a really sad statement to have to make. But, I'm a realist if nothing else! If Bartlet existed in the U.S., I'd vote for him though! Actually, I wouldn't mind voting for Martin Sheen, although Uncle Marty tends to be a little left of me politically.

Gayle says that on her site — likely because of the heavy 18–24 female demographic that seems to be its most frequent visitor — Josh Lyman is a top-ranking character, although there are numerous threads on all the characters. Another trend she's noticed is the speculative pairing of different characters romantically as couples. "I am obviously not an advocate of putting characters together on TV shows," says Gayle, but many folks are. A good example of this can be found on a Web site devoted entirely to a hypothetical Josh-Donna romance: **joshanddonna.fws1.com**.

Finally, I asked Gayle about her sense, based on her experience with site visitors, of the average *West Wing* viewer. Her response was interesting:

The average ww viewer is smarter than the average bear. This is smart TV, written for intelligent people. I'm not saying that to be snotty, but it's my impression. The folks who post to the message board for the most part, are well written, well thought out people — even the younger kids who post are true of this. It's an exceptional group of people; actually it's turned into a community with over 1200 registered members who post daily. I would also think it fair to say that the average viewer is into the writing, the acting and the politics. During our recent presidential debacle, we had endless debates and threads dedicated to pure politics. It was fascinating, and for the most part, we managed to stay away from the mud slinging that takes place in most political arenas. People managed to state the opinions without turning it into a shouting match. That's indicative of a *ww* viewer I think.

The third Web-Winger I interviewed was Rachel Vagts, who hosts the **thewestwing.tktv.net** site. Vagts runs the site from her home in Iowa. It's hosted by the mega-site TKTV, home to a number of unofficial TV-show sites. Vagts used to live in DC and work in politics, so she has some particularly good insights into the show. On the Web, she'd previously run a site devoted to the series *Party of Five*, and wanted to keep her hand in the world of TV fan sites after it left the air. "You have to really love a show to keep a site running," she says, "because it takes an enormous amount of work. This is totally a pleasure job, there's no money involved and I have a separate full-time job."

One of the best things about the TKTV *West Wing* site is that it provides excellent reviews of each episode. Vagts says that she prizes these pieces as much as anything about her site. "I think that reading someone else's view on the show helps them to think more about it," she says. "*The West Wing* is a very thought-provoking show and so it's helpful to have a forum where you can exchange ideas."

Given her experience with TV-show sites, Vagts should be able to offer a good prediction about the show's future. She does, placing the fate of *The West Wing* squarely on the shoulders of its creator:

We've only seen two seasons of a series from Aaron

Nix grins with Schiff in the make-believe oval office

COURTESY SUSANNAH NIX

Sorkin (TWW and *Sports Night*) so I don't know if he suffers from the third season blahs that David E. Kelly seems to get.... I guess we could do eight seasons with a cast like this and then elect a Republican and do eight more with a totally different cast.... With the experts they have pulled together like Dee Dee Myers and Marlin Fitzwater they should have enough stories to keep going for a long while.... I will say that I've heard comments that there has been a sophomore slump to the show, that plots from *Sports Night* have shown up on the new show. I don't see the slump, and while there have been some similarities, there are a great number of people who didn't see *Sports Night* and the plots have worked well on TWW.

Finally, Vagts made an interesting point about one of her main criticisms of the show:

> [T]hat Sorkin has made his female characters look foolish; Donna has her name sewn in her underwear that somehow land on the floor of a party, C.J. sits in wet paint, Ainsley gets drunk and meets the President in her bathrobe. . . . Aaron responded to these criticisms on a public message board. He pointed out that we're very quick to criticize female characters. They have to be strong all of the time. I thought about that, thought about all the stupid things Josh and Sam have done (like trying to burn down the White House) and realized Sorkin was right. It's just like female politicians. They have to be so much better, free from any type of scandal while we revere male politicians who cheat on their wives, drive drunk, commit fraud, etc.

The fourth *West Wing* Web denizen I spoke to was Susannah Nix, host of the **www.jedbartlet.com** site. Nix, who runs the site from her home in Texas, previously worked in Web design and marketing. She says that as a stay-at-home mom, operating the site gives her an opportunity to keep active in her field. She's also been trying her hand at writing TV scripts, and says that keeping closely connected with *The West Wing* via her work on the site gives her the kind of stimulation and up-close look at a quality show she needs.

Here's how Nix explains the reason for the show's popularity:

> Television professionals get paid lots of money to try and figure this kind of thing out, but I'll take a whack at it and offer my laywoman's opinion. I guess the

It's meet-the-president time for Nix as she stops for a chat with Sheen

COURTESY SUSANNAH NIX

thing that stands out most about *The West Wing* is the writing. It's intelligent, fresh, witty, and doesn't fall into the typical television traps of cliché and predictability. And it achieves an appealing balance between humor and drama that totally sucks you in. I also think people respond to a show that doesn't talk down to them and isn't afraid to present intelligent subject matter. It manages to educate without preaching and I really think that's struck a chord with the audience. Watching *The West Wing* makes you want to be a better citizen. I know of a lot of people who've looked deeper into the issues presented on the show, or started volunteering for causes in their community. And many students have chosen to pursue political science because of interests that have been awakened by *The West Wing*. It dramatizes the behind-the-scenes battles that you don't get to see on the nightly news. There's been a lot of disillusionment with the political process in the U.S. lately, and *The West Wing* reminds us that there's still a lot to admire about our government.

Nix then offered her opinion on what kind of person visits a site like hers:

They're mostly (but certainly not all) women and seem to encompass all ages. I've encountered fans as young as 11 and as old as 60. There is a strong contingent of school-age fans (high school and college), as well as a lot of 20- and 30-somethings. I'd say on average *West Wing* fans tend to be educated, intelligent, and interested in learning more about the issues presented on the show. As you might expect they generally fall on the left end of the political spectrum, but I've encountered a surprising number of conservatives who love the show. I've seen some of the most passionate, thought-provoking, and amazingly civil debates on politics and current events in *West Wing* forums.

Nix also had good things to say about the way visitors to her site react to the various characters on the show:

Each character has his/her own devoted fan base. Part of the appeal of the show is that it's such an amazing ensemble, with brilliant actors and intricately developed characters. If I had to pick one as the most popular I guess it's probably Josh. His female followers, known as the Harem, have dedicated themselves to the worship of Joshuagoodness, which involves lots of swooning at the sight of his swagger and dimples. Toby is also incredibly popular. You've never seen so many women go weak in the knees at the sight of a middle-aged, grumpy bald man as in *West Wing* fandom. It's interesting that Rob Lowe was expected to be the heart-throb but I'd say Josh and Toby each leave a much larger swath of lovelorn female fans in their wake than Sam, although he's certainly got his fair share. C.J. is pretty much unanimously worshipped by everyone. Obviously everyone loves Bartlet, as well as Leo and Charlie. The recurring characters also have a huge fan base. Mrs. Landingham is wildly popular, but the other assistants, Bonnie, Ginger, and Carol, and even Larry and Ed, have their own cheering sections.

Nix is something of a legend among *West Wing* fans because she's actually visited the show's set — thanks to winning an online charity auction. She met most of the cast, as well as Aaron Sorkin, Thomas Schlamme, Llewellyn Wells, and director Clark Johnson. She even had three walk-ons in the "Six Meetings Before Lunch" episode. Although the trip is described in loving detail on her site I wanted her overall feelings about getting a chance that very, very few fans ever get:

> More than anything, I think it illustrated what a special show this is. Everyone I met seemed to be genuinely proud to be working there. I was fortunate to visit during the first season, before the big Emmy win and the huge jump in the ratings. People were just starting to realize that the show was a hit and were excited to be involved with it. You hear so many stories about how

cutthroat and competitive Hollywood is, but every single person I met was incredibly kind. I spent two full days on the set working as a member of the background and I didn't see any displays of ego or lack of respect for anyone else. The cast and crew were all very generous with their time and did their best to make me feel welcome. It was an amazing experience that just heightened my respect for the show.

Nix's site also contains a good bit of *West Wing* "fanfic," which essentially involves taking characters from an established show and writing stories with them as lead characters. Although Nix said she would likely be taking down this part of the site before this book was published, it does illustrate a whole new element of fandom.

Nix's final question was a two-parter. How did she and the visitors to her site compare the first two seasons of the show? And how do they think it has changed during the 44 episodes aired to date?

There's a prevailing sense among viewers who've been around for both seasons that last year was better. My personal opinion is that there's really no way for a show to live up to the expectations set by a great first season. It's like the beginning of a romance, where everything is exciting and new, and then you settle into a deeper, more comfortable relationship where there are good days and bad days. If you go back and watch any favorite show, there's going to be a special nostalgia for the first season episodes and I don't think the subsequent seasons can be judged against them fairly. My favorite *West Wing* episodes are the first six, but this season has had plenty of fantastic episodes.

Some people seem to think the second season has been darker than the first, but I think there's always been a lot of darkness in the show. I got so sick of all the press last year describing the show as an "idealistic" portrayal of the presidency. Now I think people are discovering that that's really not what it's about. From the beginning, the characters have been flawed and I don't think they're any more noble than the average public servant. The thing that's great about this show is that it illustrates how easy it is for people with good intentions to get so caught up in the game of politics that they lose their way.

CHAPTER FIVE

THE CAST

Part One: The Recurring Characters

Although *The West Wing* has reaped much praise from fans and critics for its superb ensemble starring cast, the show has also drawn raves for its excellent group of recurring characters — people who appear with enough regularity to warrant the moniker. Some of them are seen frequently as employees of the White House; others visit *The West Wing* as politicians, family members of the staff, foreign dignitaries, or folks connected with American politics and the President in some way.

The following is a look at two dozen of these recurring characters, some background on the actors who play them, and details about the characters themselves.

Actor: John Amos, born December 27, 1939 in Newark, New Jersey
Bio Highlights: Regular on three other TV series: *The District* as Mayor Ethan

Baker (2000–present), *Good Times* as James Evans (1974–76), *The Mary Tyler Moore Show*, as Gordon (Gordy) Howard (1970–73)
Character: Percy Fitzwallace, U.S. Navy Admiral

John Amos, who most people recall as the dour dad on the series *Good Times*, has appeared as Chairman of the Joint Chiefs of Staff, Admiral Percy Fitzwallace, in four episodes during season one. After Aaron Sorkin was criticized for the lack of minority characters in the pilot episode, he made assurances there would soon be people of color in important positions in subsequent episodes — and Fitzwallace was one of them. He provided ongoing key military advice to president Bartlet and advised Leo about hiring Charlie Young, when Leo expressed concern that a young black man carrying the president's bags might look bad. Fitzwallace was one of the 14 people who knew about the president's MS before the end of season one.

Actor: Timothy Busfield, born June 12, 1957 in Lansing, Michigan
Bio Highlights: Eliot Weston on TV series *thirtysomething* (1987–91), Dr. John "J.T." McIntyre on TV series *Trapper John, M.D.* (1984–86)
Character: Danny Concannon, White House reporter, *Washington Post*

Timothy Busfield is one of those actors you just can't seem to separate from a seminal role from early in their career — in his case it was his portrayal of the slightly neurotic advertising exec Eliot Weston on *thirtysomething*. Busfield landed himself a plum role on *The West Wing* as Danny Concannon, a *Washington Post* reporter who seems to have the best access to many of the stories emanating from the White House, due mainly to his close relationship with C.J. Cregg. Lots of sub-plot time was given over to the potential romance between Danny and C.J. in season one, with both parties wondering if it was ethical for a White House press secretary to date a reporter. The wise-cracking Danny, who's also reported on Washington politics for the *New York Times*, *Time* magazine, and the *Dallas Morning News* ultimately decided to cool things with C.J., and even turned down a desk-editor's position (which

Timothy Busfield's Danny Concannon character started off strong on The West Wing *but found his screen time cut way back during Season Two*

GARY MARSHALL/
SHOOTING STAR

presumably would have meant that he'd be able to date C.J. freely), saying that he was a reporter first and foremost. Although Danny was a regular visitor in season one, he appeared very sparingly in the second season. "I was in 14 episodes the first season and four this season," Busfield told USA *Today* during the 2001 summer show hiatus. "Based on that, I'll probably be in one next year."

Actor: Stockard Channing, born February 13, 1944
Bio Highlights: Co-star, *Grease* (1978), *Six Degrees of Separation* (1993), TV series *Stockard Channing in Just Friends* (1979), *The Stockard Channing Show* (1980)
Character: First Lady Dr. Abigail (Abby) Bartlet, MD

One of the major recurring characters, Dr. Bartlet — under relentless questioning by Chief White House counsel Oliver Babish late in season two, she insisted on being called "Dr. Bartlet," wondering aloud, "When the hell did it become Mrs. Bartlet?" — holds an MD from Harvard, has been practicing medicine for 26 years, and specializes in Internal Medicine and Thoracic Surgery. She is also an adjunct professor of thoracic surgery at Harvard Medical School and a member of the staff of Boston Mercy Hospital and Columbia Presbyterian Medical Center. She has been married to Jed Bartlet for 33 years and has three daughters (Liz, Ellie, and Zoey) and one granddaughter (Annie). Veteran actress Stockard Channing, who's best remembered from her role as Rizzo in *Grease,* was surprised to be offered the role of the First Lady before season one began, but has shone in the part. She's the perfect pragmatic foil to the quirky president, and her knowledge of his medical condition coupled with her desire that he forego a run for a second term in office has made for some arresting drama.

Actor: Lisa Edelstein, born May 21, 1967 in Boston, Massachusetts
Bio Highlights: *What Women Want* (2000), TV series *Sports Night* (1999) as Bobbie Bernstein, *Relativity* (1996–97) as Rhonda Roth
Character: Laurie, a Georgetown University law student; a.k.a. Brittany Rollins, a call girl

Despite the many protestations that *The West Wing* is just a TV show, if anyone wanted to take a shot at it for being a little unrealistic at times, the character of Laurie (or her *nom de guerre* Brittany Rollins) would be a good place to start. While it's possible that some George Washington University Law School grads may have worked their way through school as high-priced call girls, it's highly unlikely. Still, it's hard not to see the attractive Laurie as a kind of mirror to the soul of Sam Seaborn — through her, we get to see some of Sam's core traits: his vulnerability, sense of humor, and, above all, his strange occasional lack of judgment when his career is at stake. Laurie is played by Lisa Edelstein, who appeared on Sorkin's earlier primetime series, *Sports Night.*

Actor: Renée Estevez
Bio Highlights: *Addams Family Reunion* (1998), *Good Girls Don't* (1993)
Character: Nancy, secretary to presidential secretary, Dolores Landingham

Martin Sheen and wife Janet's only daughter — her siblings include brothers Carlos (Charlie Sheen), Emilio, and Ramon — Renée Estevez plays Nancy, assistant to Mrs. Landingham. Following Mrs. L's tragic departure at the end of the second season, it will be interesting to see what happens to Nancy in season three.

Actor: Melissa Fitzgerald
Bio Highlights: *Frequency* (2000), *Love & Sex* (2000)
Character: Carol, secretary to press secretary C.J. Cregg

Carol appears constantly at press secretary C.J. Cregg's side during high-pressure press briefings, and often remains at the podium after C.J. has left, telling journalists that more information will be forthcoming when available, etc. She's often responsible for keeping C.J. sane (or at least semi-organized) during particularly hectic moments.

Actor: Jorja Fox, born July 7, 1968 in New York City
Bio highlights: TV series *ER*, as Dr. Margaret "Maggie" Doyle (1996–99); *Memento* (2000)
Character: Gina Toscano, secret service agent; bodyguard of Zoey Bartlet

President Bartlet hired 27-year-old secret service agent Gina Toscano as personal bodyguard for his daughter Zoey late in season one, after Zoey began receiving death threats from white supremacists because of her relationship with Charlie, and a racially motivated incident at a Washington bar. Toscano had a year and a half of special training for the assignment, but admitted that she was most happy when Zoey decided to spend her free time in her dorm room eating pizza and watching a movie. Toscano felt considerable guilt over the shooting that closed season one, but was assured that she'd done her job well.

Actor: Kathryn Joosten
Bio highlights: Numerous TV series guest appearances including *ER* (1996), *Murphy Brown* (1996), *Frasier* (1997), *Seinfeld* (1997), *Dharma & Greg* (1998), *Providence* (1999), *Becker* (2000), *Buffy the Vampire Slayer* (2000), and many others
Character: Mrs. Dolores Landingham (deceased), secretary to President Bartlet (** The role of young Mrs. Landingham was played by Kirsten Nelson in Episode 44's flashback scenes)

We learned more about Mrs. L. in the final show of season two than we had in all 43 previous episodes combined. Using a series of flashbacks, Sorkin reconstructed the first meeting of Jed Bartlet and Mrs. Landingham, back in the 1960s when young Jed was a student at a New England prep school, and Mrs. L. was his father's (who was the school headmaster) assistant.

The thirty-something Landingham was played by a much younger actress named Kirsten Nelson in the flashbacks. Joosten explained at a June 2001 Toronto press tour that she and Nelson worked very closely in getting the older woman's mannerisms and speech patterns just right — and there was general agreement that Nelson's portrayal of the young Mrs. L. was flawless.

Mrs. L. became a beloved character from the early episodes because of her crusty, no-nonsense attitude — especially when bantering with the president. We also learned about a personal tragedy — twin sons who were killed in Vietnam. But saddest of all was her sudden death in episode 43. After most of the hour-long episode had featured a sub-plot that centered on her finally having bought a brand-new car, she was struck by a drunk driver and killed while driving back to the White House.

It wasn't the end of things for Mrs. L., however. In the next episode, she appeared as a ghost — with the same crusty but lovable personality — to advise Bartlet on whether or not he should run again. And it seems as though it's still not over for Mrs. Landingham, as all signs point to her re-appearing in season three in subsequent ghostly visitations. When she was in Toronto for the Canadian press tour, actress Joosten admitted that she was not sure just how the scenes would be constructed (Sorkin's habitual last-minute script deliveries usually means no one in the cast knows what's going to happen in the next episode) but that she's ready to make more appearances.

A discussion of Mrs. L. would be incomplete without learning a bit about the woman who plays her. Kathryn Joosten began her working life as a psychiatric nurse in Chicago before marrying a psychiatrist and raising two sons. When her marriage broke up, Joosten found herself a single mother trying to support her two boys. She decided to pursue her dream of becoming an actress, and appeared in local plays. That led to a stint as a street performer at Walt Disney World and MGM studios in Orlando, Florida. When one of her boys moved to L.A. to further his career in music, Joosten decided to accompany him. After landing a part on the series *Family Matters* in 1996, Joosten started securing parts in plays, commercials, movies, drama series, and sitcoms. Even though she was in her 60s, this "beginner" actor had finally realized her dream — with her role on *The West Wing* putting the icing on the cake.

Actor: Charley Lang, born December 24, 1955 in Passaic, New Jersey
Bio highlights: TV series, *Dark Skies* as Dr. Halligan (1996)
Character: Matt Skinner, congressman

To the amazement of many West Wing staffers — particularly Josh Lyman — Republican member of Congress Matt Skinner supports the Marriage Recognition Act, which would prohibit gay marriages but is gay himself. Skinner also sits on the Commerce Committee that is opposed to the confusing (at least by C.J. and Sam's admission) practice of statistical sampling in the census.

Actor: John Larroquette, born November 25, 1947 in New Orleans
Bio highlights: TV series *Night Court* (1984–92), *The John Larroquette Show* (1993)
Character: Lionel Tribbey, White House Counsel

Veteran actor John Larroquette is indelibly linked with his longtime role on the series *Night Court* — a role for which he won four straight best supporting comedy actor Emmys in the 1980s, before asking to have his name removed from any subsequent nominee's lists. He only appeared in one episode of *The West Wing* (hardly a "recurring" role) as Lionel Tribbey, Bartlet's fourth White House Counsel, but he made such an impact that he's been included here. Tribbey was the strong-willed White House Counsel who appeared in Episode 27 ("And It's Surely to Their Credit") as the fellow who fired those two staffers for putting the "Bitch" notice and dead flowers on Ainsley Hayes's basement desk, and who does not suffer fools gladly. It's not likely that Tribbey will be making any more appearances on *The West Wing* — as least not as General Counsel — since Oliver Babish took over that position late in season two.

Actor: Tim Matheson, born December 31, 1947 in Glendale, California
Bio highlights: *National Lampoon's Animal House* (1978), *Divorce American Style* (1967), *Fletch* (1989)
Character: Vice President John Hoynes

If you wanted to make a solid argument that *The West Wing* is not a reality-based TV series, Vice President John Hoynes might be a good place to start. He and President Bartlet, it's safe to say, do *not* get along — when else in U.S. political history have the president and the VP shared such mutual antipathy? Played by veteran actor Tim Matheson (who will always be etched in many TV watchers' brains as Otter, one of the zany frat brothers on *Animal House*), VP

Hoynes has repeatedly suggested that he'll be the next president, and that Bartlet wouldn't have been elected without his help. It's true that Bartlet did enlist the help of the Texan Hoynes to carry several key states, but it's unclear what Hoynes's political future will be in the wake of Bartlet's MS disclosure. It's also worth noting that Josh Lyman was once heavily involved in Hoynes's campaign before switching allegiances to Bartlet, at the urgings of his friend Sam and Leo McGarry.

Actor: Marlee Matlin, born August 24, 1965 in Morton Grove, Illinois
Bio highlights: *Children of a Lesser God* (1986 — won an Academy Award for Best Actress)
Character: Political consultant Joey Lucas

Easily one of the more popular characters on *The West Wing*, political consultant Joey Lucas is savvy, sexy — and deaf. Lucas communicates via sign language through her interpreter Kenny, but also speaks on occasion, especially when she wants to make a point. Of course, it would be impossible to talk about Joey Lucas without making reference to the romantic sub-plot involving her and Josh Lyman. It's been clear since early in the first season that Josh — despite his tendency to insult her — has been infatuated with her, but her relationship with pollster Al Keifer put a temporary end to that. When he discovered that the two were no longer involved, Josh was ready to pursue Lucas again, but the two never did get together. Romance aside, Lyman paid Lucas the ultimate professional compliment when he asked her to conduct a poll to gauge public reaction to a hypothetical situation (an imaginary congressman from Michigan who lied about a serious personal medical problem) in order to project Bartlet's chances for re-election.

Actor: Elisabeth Moss, born 1983 in Los Angeles
Bio highlights: *Girl, Interrupted* (1999), *Anywhere But Here* (1999)
Character: Zoey Bartlet, the President's daughter

The introduction of Zoey Bartlet — youngest of the president's daughters — early in season one set the stage for two major character and plot developments. The first was the opportunity to see the president in the role of a father. Early episodes amply illuminated Bartlet's role as a statesman and President — now viewers would be able to see how he fared as a dad, especially one of a semi-rebellious college student. Also, Zoey's influence on the overall dramatic arc of *The West Wing* was apparent in her relationship with Charlie Young — and the predictable yet increasingly ominous reaction from white supremacist groups, which culminated in the shooting scene ending season one.

Actor: Suzy Nakamura
Bio highlights: *Daddio* (2000) TV series
Character: Kathy, Deputy Communications Director Sam Seaborn's secretary

Kathy (last name unknown) has been Sam Seaborn's assistant since the pilot episode. Like many of the administrative assistants on the show, she appears only sporadically, usually in non-speaking segments or segments when she speaks only briefly. She's been known to steal donuts from Sam's desk.

Actor: Bill O'Brien
Bio highlights: Guest appearance, *Gideon's Crossing* (2001) TV series
Character: Kenny Thurman, assistant to Joey Lucas

Kenny first showed up beside Joey Lucas in episode 16 — and has shared every one of her appearances since then as her sign-language interpreter except one, when he was on vacation.

Actor: Michael O'Neil
Character: Secret Service Director Ron Butterfield

Ron Butterfield heads up President Bartlet's Secret Service team. He played a key role in the season one finale / season two opener, when he was shot in the right hand during the attempt on Charlie Young's life by white supremacists. He also made a point of assuring Toby Zeigler that despite Toby's suggestion that Bartlet walk in the open and uncovered to public appearances, the president's security was maintained at maximum levels at all times, assuring his safety — and relieving Toby of a truckload of guilt.

Actor: Devikah Parikh
Bio highlights: Guest appearances, TV series *Frasier* (2001), *Chicago Hope* (1997)
Character: Bonnie, a communications aide to Toby Zeigler

One of Toby's communications assistants, Bonnie has appeared in a total of 14 episodes during the first and second seasons, earning her mention in this section.

Actor: Oliver Platt, born January 12, 1960 in Washington D.C.
Bio highlights: TV series *Deadline* (2000); *Ready to Rumble* (2000), *The Three Musketeers* (1993)
Character: White House Counsel Oliver Babish

The no-BS White House Counsel Oliver Babish was brought in for the final four episodes of season two to begin building a defence for president Bartlet and any staffers who may have committed fraud after learning that the president had MS and remaining mum. Babish is played by Oliver Platt, whose own father was an American diplomat who held several overseas postings. After his introduction in episode 41 in which he grilled the president and Leo, Babish went all out in the following installment, questioning staff members one by one in a marathon session.

Actor: Emily Procter
Bio highlights: *Submerged*, TV-movie (2001)
Character: Associate White House Counsel Ainsley Hayes

Ainsley Hayes is one of those recurring characters — like Mrs. Landingham — who verges on becoming a regular cast member. She was brought in early in season two when she was hired by Leo and Bartlet as an associate White House counsel after holding her own against Sam on a televised debate. A Harvard Law School graduate, Ainsley's grandfather once served as the chairman of the North Carolina Republican party, and she herself is a die-hard Republican, which makes for all kinds of interesting situations when she engages in political debates with Sam and other White House staffers. The Ainsley character can be seen as a symbol of the kind of informed patriotism that suffuses and animates most of the characters on *The West Wing*. Although she's a loyal Republican in a sea of Democrats, Ainsley is deeply committed to non-partisan democratic principles and the American form of government. This, of course, has not delivered her from her miserable basement office, or from getting drunk and embarrassing herself by dancing in her bathrobe in front of the president the first time she met him at the White House.

Actor: Roger Rees, born May 5, 1944, in Aberystwyth, Wales
Bio highlights: TV series *Cheers* (1989–91), *A Christmas Carol* (1987)
Character: Lord John Marbury, British Ambassador to the United States

Most people who watch TV recognize English actor Roger Rees from his role as snooty corporate banker Robin Colcord on *Cheers*. But on *The West Wing* Rees has appeared three times as the equally abrasive and erratically brilliant Lord John Marbury. He was initially invited to Washington to settle a potentially explosive border dispute between India and Pakistan, and was later elevated to the post of British ambassador to the U.S. As well as being an excellent diplomat, Marbury is a well-known and avid skirt-chaser and prodigious drinker. He has no greater rival in Washington than Leo McGarry — his polar opposite in just about every way imaginable.

Actor: Nicole Robinson
Bio highlights: *Any Given Sunday* (1999)
Character: Margaret, secretary to White House Chief of Staff Leo McGarry

Margaret once confessed to her boss that she'd become pretty good at forging the president's signature — an ability that Leo discouraged her from improving upon. Margaret is usually summoned not by the intercom, but by Leo bellowing out her name. Despite Leo's irascibility, Margaret clearly feels concern and compassion for him — she expressed serious misgivings to staff members that Leo might begin drinking again on the day his divorce became final.

Actor: Allison Smith, born December 9, 1969, in New York City
Bio highlights: Guest spots on *Murder, She Wrote* (1984), *Beverly Hills, 90210* (1990), *Sweet Justice* (1994), *Homicide: Life on the Street* (1993), *Touched by an Angel* (1994)
Character: Mallory O'Brien, grade school teacher and daughter of Leo McGarry

If for no other reason, Mallory O'Brien will be forever remembered among fans of *The West Wing* as the teacher in charge of the class trip to the White House in the pilot episode. It was the class Sam Seaborn completely embarrassed himself in front of by his lack of knowledge of the history of the White House, and then completed his humiliation by telling her (before he found out she was Leo's daughter) that he'd unknowingly slept with a prostitute. As might be expected, she soon struck up a romance with Sam, which lead to tensions between her and her father, who concocted all kinds of schemes to keep the two apart. In the aftermath of her parents' separation early in season one, Mallory also played an important part in keeping her dad sane and maintaining some contact with family life.

Actor: Anna Deveare Smith, born September 18, 1950 in Baltimore, Maryland
Character Position:
Bio highlights: *Twilight: Los Angeles* (2000), stage play adapted for TV on PBS; *The American President* (1995)
Character: National Security Advisor Nancy McNally

National Security Adviser Nancy McNally appears in crucial situations to advise President Bartlet and staff on matters of national defence. She first appeared in the second season opener, and was a key figure in the confusion following the shooting about who was in charge of the country while Bartlet's condition remained unclear. Veteran actor Anna Deveare Smith, who played a leading role in Sorkin's *The American President*, also won fame for her performance in the 2000 PBS adaptation of *Twilight: Los Angeles*, a one-woman show she'd been performing on stage since 1996. The play dealt with her description of the Rodney King riots in Los Angeles in 1992.

Actor: Kim Webster
Character: Ginger, secretary to Communications Director Toby Zeigler

A native of New Jersey, Ginger occasionally has to bear the brunt of her boss's tirades. Hers is another part with very few lines, but frequent appearances. She appeared in a total of 14 episodes during the first and second seasons.

CHAPTER SIX

THE CAST

Part Two: The Stars

Although *The West Wing* is home to more than 30 characters of varying political stripes and importance to the 44 plotlines aired to date, there are nine who have emerged as show "regulars." In other words, these are the stars of *The West Wing*.

They include Martin Sheen (as President Josiah Bartlet) and the members of his immediate staff who were billed as series' stars when the show launched in 1999: John Spencer (Leo McGarry), Rob Lowe (Sam Seaborn), Bradley Whitford (Josh Lyman), Richard Schiff (Toby Zeigler), and Allison Janney (C.J. Cregg).

Dulé Hill joined the staff as Bartlet's young aide, Charlie Young, in the third episode, and also achieved star billing. Although Janel Moloney, who plays Josh Lyman's secretary, Donna Moss, was not billed as a series star in season one, she did reach that plateau in the second season.

As a footnote, Moira Kelly appeared in NBC press material and the show's opening credits as a co-star in the first season, in the role of the political consultant Mandy Hampton. As we saw in chapter two, however, Kelly did not return for *The West Wing*'s second season.

The following are brief sketches of each of *The West Wing*'s main characters and the actors who play them.

☆

Actor: Martin Sheen, born Ramon Estevez on August 3, 1940, in Dayton, Ohio **(In the second-season finale the high-school-aged Bartlet was played in flashback sequences by Jason Widener)
Character: Josiah (Jed) Bartlet, President

Actor Bio:
Martin Sheen was born the seventh of 10 children to a Salvadoran immigrant family in Dayton, Ohio — he changed his name in the 1960s to overcome the stigma against Latino actors, choosing "Sheen" in honor of the famous Catholic archbishop, J. Fulton Sheen. Despite the name change, he's always been a vocal champion for Hispanic actors in Hollywood, and he's won several awards from Latino organizations in recognition of his leadership and talents.

Hollywood legend has it that Sheen failed his entrance exam to the University of Dayton so he could pursue acting — a choice his father vehemently opposed.

Sheen has been married to Janet Templeton since 1961, and their four children — Charlie Sheen, Emilio Estevez, Renée Estevez, and Ramon Estevez — are all actors — as is Sheen's brother, Joe Estevez. The most notable family collaboration came in the 1987 movie *Wall Street*, in which Charlie playing an up-and-coming stock trader, and Martin his hard-working, union-organizing dad. Charlie and Martin crossed paths again beginning in 2000 on Wednesday nights during prime time when Charlie replaced Michael J. Fox on ABC's *Spin City*, while his father continued his Bartlet role on NBC.

The elder Sheen has never been one to shy away from controversy — having been arrested more than 60 times during a protest career that's

Long an avid political activist, Martin Sheen brings a presence to the Bartlet character that's at the very heart of the show

YORAM KANANA/SHOOTING STAR

spanned five decades. He's an especially vocal opponent of the School Of The Americas, a U.S. military base that trains Latin American soldiers, and has played a part in annual protests at the base since 1998.

Sheen has also been equally candid about his personal problems. A recovering alcoholic, he's spoken numerous times about his attempts to overcome his addiction, as well as his efforts to help son Charlie with his own drug and alcohol problems. During the marathon, year-long shooting of the 1979 movie *Apocalypse Now* (in which Sheen stars as a U.S. Army captain sent into the Cambodian jungle to capture a rebel colonel played by Marlon Brando), Sheen suffered a heart attack and a nervous breakdown while on location in the Philippines. He describes these traumatic experiences in the 1991 documentary, *Hearts of Darkness: A Filmmaker's Apocalypse*. After making a full recovery, Sheen experienced another dramatic event during the filming of 1982's *Gandhi*, when he met Mother Teresa, and returned to his Roman Catholic roots.

Sheen has appeared in more than 130 films and TV movies, including 1968's *The Subject Was Roses* — adapted from the Broadway play he also starred in. In 1973, he enjoyed a minor breakthrough in the role of a disillusioned murderer in the film *Badlands*, and then reached the big time in *Apocalypse Now*. On TV, he's starred in *The Execution of Private Slovik* (1974), the miniseries *Kennedy* (1983), and *The Missiles of October* (1974). Sheen was also a popular character on the soap *As The World Turns* in the 1960s and '70s. Sheen joined the cast of *The West Wing* because of Aaron Sorkin and John Wells — he'd worked with Sorkin in his role as presidential advisor A.J. McInerney in *The American President* — and received an Emmy nomination in the show's first season. In 2001, Sheen won a Golden Globe for Best Performance by an Actor in a TV Series Drama.

Character Bio:
The cornerstone of *The West Wing*, President Bartlet is at turns deeply compassionate and emphatically hot-headed. He's in his late-50s, and, no matter what the critics might say about *The West Wing*'s overall liberal bias, really is a Democrat's dream president. He is faithfully married — no Clintonesque scandals in *this* White House! — to Dr. Abigail (Abby) Bartlet, and the couple has three daughters: Elizabeth (who has a 12-year-old daughter, Annie, making the First Couple grandparents as well), Ellie (a medical student), and Zoey (who is in college at nearby Georgetown).

Bartlet grew up as the son of a private-school headmaster, and is a staunch Catholic. Details on his mother are sketchy, but we do know that he inherited his Catholicism from her. He claims that his great-great grandfather was one of the original signatories of the Declaration of Independence.

Bartlet attended Notre Dame University in South Bend, Indiana, and remains a fervent supporter of the Fighting Irish football team. He has joked that in his youth, he'd considered becoming a priest. An economist by trade, Bartlet holds a PhD and won the Nobel Prize in that discipline. Unlike his right-hand man and best friend Leo McGarry, Bartlet has never served in the military. He was a two-term Governor of New Hampshire, and a three term congressman from that state.

Bartlet has been battling multiple sclerosis for the past two years, and his decision to disclose his condition to the nation was a crucial sub-plot to the final episodes of season two. He's a reformed smoker but still sneaks a couple of cigarettes a day outside the White House.

He's a basketball fan, enjoys playing tennis and chess, and apparently also likes bicycle riding, although he injured himself while cycling during the pilot episode and has apparently never tried it since.

What the actor says:

About his name change: "I've been an actor for 40 years. . . . I've played all kinds of parts. I'm Hispanic by birth and I'm Irish by trade." (NBC Summer Press Tour, July 1999, Los Angeles)

About his alcoholism: "Personally, I'm in the program, the AA program. I've been sober, thank God, for 12 years, and I'm a grateful alcoholic." (Toronto *Globe and Mail*, November 16, 2000)

About his personal politics: "If a Republican showed me a heart, I'd respond to that heart. I have not seen too much heart coming from Republicans." (*George*, November 2000)

What his character says:

About his political acumen: "I've never lost an election in my life." (Episode 20, "Mandatory Minimums")

About his informal way of dealing with his staff: "Jokes are part of my folksy charm. . . . It's at the heart of my popularity." (Episode 2, "Post Hoc, Ergo Propter Hoc")

About his desire to renounce religion on the eve of Mrs.

Landingham's funeral and his disclosure to the nation that he has MS (Bartlet makes the impassioned speech in Latin): "Am I really to believe that these are the acts of a loving God? A just God? A wise God? To hell with Your punishments! I was Your servant here on Earth. And I spread Your word and I did Your work. To hell with your punishments. To hell with you. [Then in English] You get Hoynes!" (Episode 44, "Two Cathedrals")

☆

Actor: Rob Lowe, born March 17, 1964 in Charlottesville, Virginia
Character: Deputy Communications Director Sam Seaborn

Actor Bio:
Like co-stars Martin Sheen and Allison Janney, Rob Lowe grew up in Dayton, Ohio (although he was born in Virginia). Lowe was a member of the notorious "Brat Pack" in the 1980s — which also included brothers and sons of Martin Sheen, Emilio Estevez and Charlie Sheen — after getting his start in acting and modeling as a kid. Lowe's Brat Pack-era movies included *Class* and *The Outsiders* (both 1983), *Oxford Blues* and *The Hotel New Hampshire* (1984), *St. Elmo's Fire* (1985), *Youngblood* (1986), *Square Dance* (1987), and *Masquerade* (1988).

Lowe's career took a pounding in 1989 when news surfaced of a sex videotape he made with two women — one of them underage at the time — at the 1988 Democratic convention in Atlanta. Lowe settled the case out of court with the minor's family, and performed 20 hours of community service in Dayton. Around the same time, he began to seek help for a serious drug and alcohol problem which he eventually overcame.

Lowe married a former makeup artist named Sheryl Berkoff in 1991, and the couple have two sons. Lowe's brother Chad is also an actor, and in 1993 won an Emmy for playing a young man with AIDS on the popular series *Life Goes On*. Chad Lowe's wife is the Oscar-winning actress Hilary Swank.

As Sam Seaborn, Rob Lowe brings equal parts sex appeal and nerdish charm to the White House communications efforts

PAUL FENTON/SHOOTING STAR

Lowe's career was resurrected in the early 1990s, in part because friend and fellow actor Mike Myers realized that Lowe could act equally well in funny parts as well as dramatic ones. Myers cast Lowe in 1992's *Wayne's World* and in *Austin Powers II* (1999).

Lowe brings a near-lifetime on interest in politics to his role on *The West Wing.* A self-confessed "political junkie," Lowe (like Aaron Sorkin) supported George McGovern in his 1972 presidential bid — he sold cookies and lemonade to raise money for the Minnesota governor. He has been active in Democratic party politics since the 1980s. Sorkin was initially unsure that Lowe would fit in with the ensemble cast until the actor's first audition. "With very good-looking men, you're suspect of their acting abilities," Sorkin recounted to *People* magazine, just before the start of *The West Wing*'s second season. "Particularly when Rob led a career in his 20s that had a lot to do with the way he looked. But moments after his audition began, that was the last thing I was thinking." *People* also reported that Lowe was raking in about $100,000 per episode.

Character Bio:

As Deputy Communications Director, Sam Seaborn does a lot of speech-writing for the president. In his middle thirties, Seaborn left a high-paying position ($400,000 a year) at the law firm of Gage Whitney Page in New York at the urging of Josh Lyman, to come to work for Bartlet's campaign, where, as he once quipped, "any kid with a good paper route" earned more money than he did. Seaborn is a graduate of Princeton and Duke Law School.

Although he's a brilliant speechwriter and political strategist, Seaborn has the reputation of being something of a klutz among fellow staffers and Washington colleagues. He's also prepared to argue just about any point of legislation — and just as prepared to concede well-made points by opponents in these debates.

Romantically, he had a brief fling with Laurie, who he discovered was a prostitute working her way through law school, and Mallory O'Brien, Leo McGarry's daughter.

What the actor says:

> About turning his life around in 1990: "The first epiphany I had was that I should be with Sheryl. The other was that I needed to get sober." (*People*, September 11, 2000)

> About sometimes confusing *The West Wing* on TV with the real one: "When I was doing the pilot, I would come home and watch *Crossfire* and go, 'You know you have to talk to them about that the next day.' You really get lulled into the fact that you are really working there." (NBC Press Tour, Summer 1999)

> About first hearing of a new show called *The West Wing*: "I thought,

'What's that? A spin-off from *Pensacola: Wings of Gold?*'"

What his character says:

About his job: "I argue for a living." (Episode 2, "Post Hoc, Ergo Propter Hoc")

About his secret for success: "I'm less visually observant than others, but I make up for it with cunning and guile." (Episode 41, "Bad Moon Rising")

About his views on education: "Education is the silver bullet. Education is everything. We don't need little changes. We need gigantic revolutionary changes. . . . Competition for the best teachers should be fierce. They should be getting six-figure salaries. Schools should be incredibly expensive for government and absolutely free of charge for its citizens, just like national defense." (Episode 18, "Six Meetings Before Lunch")

☆

Actor: Bradley Whitford, born October 10, 1959 in Madison, Wisconsin
Character: Josh Lyman, Deputy Chief of Staff

Actor Bio:

Bradley Whitford grew up in Madison, Wisconsin, as the youngest of five children. He attended Wesleyan University in Massachusetts, graduating in 1981, and later studied acting at Julliard. After a standout career on the stage in New York (where he became friends with Aaron Sorkin), Whitford branched out into the movies and TV.

He has appeared in films such as *Bicentennial Man* (1999), *Billy Madison* (1995), and *Revenge of the Nerds II* (1997), and was a star on the short-lived series, *The Secret Lives of Men*. Whitford also did guest stints on ER and NYPD Blue. He landed the role of Josh Lyman after Sorkin exhorted him to audition for it (for more on this, see chapter two).

On the personal side, Whitford has been married to actress Jane

*Bradley Whitford with his wife
Jane Kaczmarek*

Kaczmarek since 1992, and the couple has two children. Whitford's rise to fame on *The West Wing* dovetailed with Kaczmarek's on Fox, where she plays a manic mom on the popular series *Malcolm in the Middle*.

Character Bio:
Deputy White House Chief of Staff Joshua (Josh) Lyman hails from Connecticut. He is single, a Fulbright scholar, and a graduate of Harvard and then Yale (from Josh's comments, it seems that he likely attended Harvard undergrad and then Yale Law School).

In his mid 30s, Lyman is a hard-driving, sometimes abrasive figure, who does not seem to have many interests outside his job. Romantically, he has shown some interest in the pollster/political consultant Joey Lucas, and there is always the hint of something more than flirtatious banter between him and his assistant, Donna Moss.

Lyman is the son of a renowned Connecticut lawyer who died while Josh was working on one of Bartlet's campaigns. His grandfather was in the Birkenau concentration camp during the Second World War. His older sister died tragically in a house fire when Lyman was very young, a tragedy he survived.

Prior to joining Bartlet's staff, he was floor manager for the House Minority Whip, and Chief of Staff for Congressman Earl Brennan. He also worked on the presidential campaign of Senator John Hoynes (who became Vice President under Bartlet).

Lyman was shot and seriously wounded in the final episode of season one, and was later diagnosed with post traumatic stress disorder for which he received treatment.

What the actor says:

About his life (July 1999): "There's a lot going on right now. I have a 20-month-old daughter, another baby on the way, we're renovating our house, and I'm going to work on *The West Wing.*" (NBC press kit)

About the perils of his profession: "The reason actors are basically alcoholics waiting to happen is that if you are the personality that at some point in your life goes to a Broadway play or sees a movie and somewhere in your mind you're thinking, I should be there. I should be up on screen. I should be someone that people go to see in a play — if you are that kind of person . . . then you are in the most assertive, extroverted .022 percent of the population. That's a very assertive chord in your personality. Then the business renders you totally passive. And there is no resolution to that." (*Esquire,* May 2001)

About the hard-earned success he and his wife now enjoy: "We've been available, sort of bouncing around, so we're very grateful. We know how difficult it is to get a callback, let alone a job, let alone a show that goes, let alone a show that people embrace. We're humbled." (*TV Times,* January 12, 2000)

What his character says:

About his role in the White House: "It bugs me when the President listens to anyone who isn't me." (Episode 7, "The State Dinner")

About opponents who might try to bait him into making him sound arrogant in a debate: "I don't need baiting for that." (Episode 1, "Pilot")

☆

Richard Schiff and wife Sheila Kelly at the 2000 Golden Globe Awards

ALEC MICHAEL/
GLOBE PHOTOS

Actor: Richard Schiff, born May 27, 1959
Character: Toby Zeigler, Communications Director

Actor Bio:
When Richard Schiff won the 2000 Emmy Award for best supporting actor in a drama series for his portrayal of Toby Zeigler, it marked the high point of a multifaceted dramatic career. Schiff began his theatrical work not as an actor, but as a director. After studying at the City College of New York, he was the founder and artistic director of the Manhattan Repertory Theater, and directed plays on and off Broadway. During this time, he directed the play *Antigone* with Angela Bassett, a recent CCNY graduate in 1983. He met his future wife, Sheila Kelley, during auditions for that play, and the couple eventually married in 1996.

Schiff finally made the plunge into acting in the mid-80s, starting off in theater. He joined Tim Robbins's renowned Actors Gang group, and ended up winning an Ovation Award for his part in the play *Urban Folktales*. Schiff has also appeared in more than 40 films, including *Seven* (1995), *Lost World* (1997), *Deep Impact* (1998), and *Living Out Loud* (1998). On television, Schiff played the popular character Barry Roth in 1996, on *Relativity*, and had guest stints on the David E. Kelley series *Ally McBeal*, *The Practice*, and *Chicago Hope*, as well as NBC's perennial hit, *ER*.

Character Bio:

Tough to guess in age (likely mid-40s), Toby Zeigler is a lifetime political strategist with a hangdog expression, known for his deadpan humor and the occasional explosion of temper. As White House Communications Director, the native New Yorker co-ordinates the presidential "spin" with C.J. Cregg and Sam Seaborn, and can often be seen polishing — and sometimes completely re-writing — Bartlet's speeches.

Zeigler appears to have spent some time in Korea as part of his military service, although he's obviously not old enough to have served in the Korean War. He is divorced from Congresswoman Andrea (Andy) Wyatt, but still wears a wedding band. Other staffers have referred to his regular attendance at synagogue on Saturday mornings. Toby once bought some stock that unexpectedly skyrocketed in value. In an attempt to quell accusations of insider-trading, he agreed to work for a year for $1.

What the actor says:

> About his inspiration for the Toby character: "I based it on my interest in old White Houses. . . . I kind of fell in love with the Truman White House. And there was a feeling about that White House that I wanted to bring to this character, like he's a bit of a throwback. . . . This character, I think, is someone who I would like to keep in the shadows within the reality that we have formulated here." (NBC Summer Press Tour, 1999).

What his character says:

> About the communications field: "The world can move, or not, by

changing some words." (Episode 5, "The Crackpots and these Women")

About staff relations: "I agree with Josh and I agree with C.J. and I agree with Sam. And you know how that makes me crazy." (Episode 1, "The Pilot")

☆

Actor: Allison Janney, born November 19, 1960 in Dayton, Ohio
Character: Press Secretary Claudia Jean (C.J.) Cregg

Actor Bio:

Allison Janney got the acting bug from her mother, who had studied at the Academy of Dramatic Arts in New York.

Janney attended Kenyon College in Ohio, and it was there that she got her first big acting break, when Kenyon graduate Paul Newman came back to the school to direct a play in which Janney was acting. Newman encouraged her to go to New York when she graduated, and to give acting a serious shot. Janney studied acting both in New York and London, England.

In theater, Janney won acclaim in the 1998 Broadway production of Arthur Miller's *A View From the Bridge*, and in the movie realm, she's starred in films such as *Big Night*, *The Ice Storm*, and *Primary Colors*. It was this last film that drew the attention of Aaron Sorkin, when he was considering her for the C.J. role on *The West Wing*. At 6 feet, many thought Janney was too tall to succeed as a mainstream actress. By winning the 2000 Emmy for Best Supporting Actress, Janney was able to prove the skeptics wrong.

In 1977, Janney suffered a serious injury to her leg — she lost more than half her blood and was in hospital for eight weeks — after crashing into a glass door at a house party. To this day, she says she reaches down to touch the scar that remains when she needs inspiration to play a tough dramatic scene.

Once told she was too tall to play anything but lesbians and aliens in Hollywood, Allison Janney has emerged as one of The West Wing's *best-loved characters*

PAUL FENTON/SHOOTING STAR

Character Bio:

When we first meet C.J. Cregg in Episode 1 ("The Pilot") she's working out on a treadmill, explaining to a good-looking guy next to her that she devotes the morning hours between 5 and 6 a.m. to herself, and to staying fit. Within seconds, though, C.J. has executed a perfect vaudevillian fall off the exercise equipment and onto the floor. And that pratfall more or less sums up her character — she's a master at handling chaotic press conferences and "media ops," but is often flustered and vulnerable behind the scenes. As the lone woman among the senior staff, she often exudes a den mother quality.

C.J. was working as a publicist — earning $550,000 a year for a Hollywood film studio before she was fired for telling one of the studio's major directors that he made terrible movies. She was immediately recruited by her old colleague Toby Zeigler for the Bartlet campaign. Although C.J. "plays" reporters and the TV media to perfection, she does have a soft spot for *Washington Post* reporter Danny Concannon, but the relationship has remained platonic because both realize a romance would be a conflict of interest.

What the actor says:

About her early days in acting: "It took me a while to get going. I'm

6 feet tall and not exactly the ingenue type." (NBC press kit)

About her interest in playing C.J.: "The script was really great and I immediately responded to the character. When I found out who was involved creatively, I knew I wanted to be a part of it." (NBC press kit).

What her character says:

About her love life: "I'm great in bed!" (Episode 31, "Galileo")

About the difficulties in handling a press conference: "I'm sorry, I can only answer about a dozen questions at once!" (Episode 44, "Two Cathedrals")

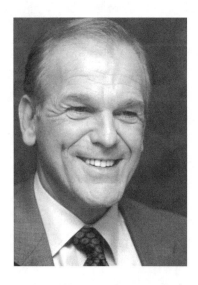

TV fans knew John Spencer best for his former role on L.A. Law, but his part as Chief of Staff Leo McGarry has really established him as a primetime presence

Actor: John Spencer, born John Speshock on December 20, 1946 in New York City
Character: Chief of Staff Leo McGarry

Actor Bio:
John Spencer grew up near Paterson, New Jersey. In 1963, the teenaged actor landed a recurring role on *The Patty Duke Show*. He followed that with a brief stint at college before dropping out to pursue an acting career. Like co-star Martin Sheen, Spencer is a recovering alcoholic, and a die-hard Democrat. He's also an avid gardener, who admitted just before the start of the 2000–01 season that his one regret in getting involved with *The West Wing* was that it was forcing him to spend less time in his garden.

Most TV fans recognize Spencer from the four seasons (1990–94) he spent on *L.A. Law* as New York attorney Tommy Mullany. He's also made guest appearances on *Law & Order*, *Miami Vice*, and *Lois & Clark: The New Adventures of Superman*, as well as the highly-regarded 1992 TV-movie, *A Jury of One*. In film, Spencer has appeared in *The Negotiator*, *Presumed Innocent*, and *The Rock*. He also has an extensive background on the stage and has continued to act in the theater since the beginning of *The West Wing*.

Character Bio:

In his late 50s, crusty Chief of Staff Leo McGarry is President Bartlet's right-hand man and is often acknowledged by Bartlet as the man who really runs the country. Divorced from ex-wife Jenny, he admits that he spent too much time on the job to maintain a marriage. His daughter, Mallory, is a teacher who was romantically involved with Sam Seaborn, which caused Leo no small consternation. His sister, Dr. Josephine McGarry, appeared in episode 30 and was considering accepting a top governmental job until the two siblings decided they'd never be able to work together.

McGarry served in Vietnam, and had previously been Secretary of Labor, likely in 1993 or 1994. He masterminded Bartlet's run for the presidency that began in 1997, and is an acknowledged recovering alcoholic and a former Valium addict — facts that were kept hidden until they were leaked by an aide. Not entirely without a sense of humor, Leo forces members of the staff to participate in an annual Big Block of Cheese Day.

What the actor says:

> About his own political views: "I am, if anything, further left than the character I play." (to Canadian interviewer Pamela Wallin)

> About giving up smoking in 1999: "It was hell on earth."
> (*Entertainment Weekly* interview)

What his character says:

> About having some justification to returning to drinking because of the pressures of his job and divorce: "I'm a recovering alcoholic, I

don't need a good reason [to drink]." (Episode 29)

About his approach to working with others: "I don't like dealing with people who are trying to impress me." (Episode 33)

About his basic nature: "I'm unpredictable." (Episode 5)

As presidential aide Charlie Young, Dulé Hill is at the center of most of the White House action

STEVEN DEFALCO/SHOOTING STAR

Actor: Dulé Hill (full name Karim Dulé Hill), born May 3, 1974

Character: Charlie Young, personal aide to President Bartlet

Actor Bio:

Dulé Hill has won as much acclaim for his skills as a tap dancer as he has for his acting. Hill was born Karim Dulé Hill, and grew up in Sayerville, NJ. He started to dance seriously at three years of age. Six years later, he appeared on Broadway in *The Tap Dance Kid*. Hill was in the 1999 movie *She's All That*, and in 1995, he brought his dance talents to the film *Bring in 'Da Noise, Bring in 'Da Funk*.

Character Bio:

Charlie Young was only 21 when he joined President Bartlet's staff as Bartlet's personal aide and assistant. Not long after, he began a romance with the president's daughter, Zoey, and the interracial nature of the relationship made him a target of white supremacist gunmen at the end of the 1999–2000 season. He hails from DC, where his mother was a police officer killed in the line of duty. Young deferred his own college entrance to support his younger sister.

What the actor says:

About his role on *The West Wing*: "There's not enough black role models on TV, and Charlie provides that." (*People*, May 22, 2000)

About his background in dance: "My mother, brother and cousin were dancing, and I just wanted to be around them . . . you can never give up the dance." (*People*)

What his character says:

About defending himself: "My philosophy of self-defense has a lot to do with running as fast as I possibly can." (Episode 41)

About his desired fate for his mother's killer: "I wouldn't want to see him executed, Mr. President. I'd want to do it myself." (Episode 14)

☆

Janel Moloney's character Donna Moss started the series as a minor player but was added to the show's main cast in the second season. So, what about her and Josh?

PAUL FENTON/SHOOTING STAR

Actor: Janel Moloney, born October 3, 1972, in Woodland Hills, California
Character: Donnatella (Donna) Moss, secretary to Deputy Chief of Staff Josh Lyman

Actor Bio:

Janel Moloney began performing at the age of five, as a ballet dancer, but quickly moved to acting. After finishing high school, she studied acting briefly at SUNY Purchase, but returned to L.A. to study with acting teacher Roy London.

Moloney appeared in a number of independent feature films, but it was her guest appearance on an episode of

Sports Night that introduced her to Aaron Sorkin. She was initially asked to audition for the role of C.J. Cregg, but ultimately landed the role of Donna Moss. Moloney's career really turned the corner in between the show's first two seasons, as she was announced as a regular on *The West Wing*.

Character Bio:

Donna Moss arrived in Washington to work on the Bartlet campaign — boldly "hiring herself" to be Josh Lyman's assistant — after two years at the University of Wisconsin. In her early or perhaps mid-20s, Moss's sarcasm and quick wit are the perfect foil for the cocky Lyman, and of course, speculation abounds about possible romantic entanglements. Her youth and inexperience occasionally makes her the butt of intra-office jokes, but Moss is more than capable of holding her own in any give-and-take verbal sparring session.

What the actor says:

About her character: "If she's not having a good time, there's something wrong. She enjoys what she does." (NBC 2000 press kit)

About Donna's walk: "You put on four-inch heels and a little tight skirt, and you're going to walk exactly the same way. . . . You've got so much to do that the last thing you can do is think about how you're walking. If you're thinking about how you're walking, you're in pretty bad shape." (NBC Summer 2000 Press Tour)

About becoming a regular on the show: "Well, I got a scooter from John Wells, which was a really great thing. . . . I feel like I've been very, very much a part of the show, both creatively and socially, since the first day." (NBC Summer 2000 Press Tour)

What her character says:

About her career and social options: "I play the flute. I'm a flautist. In high school, I was the best in my row and so I ask myself, if I pursued the flute professionally, if I'd be meeting interesting men? And the answer comes back to me: probably not." (Episode 40)

About her ability to pick men: "I have an excellent sense about these things." (Episode 40)

☆

Actor: Moira Kelly, born March 6, 1968 in Queens, New York
Character: Political Consultant Madeline (Mandy) Hampton

Actor Bio:

Moira Kelly wanted to be an actress from the time she was a youngster. The daughter of a concert pianist and a nurse, she studied acting in college and went on to roles in a number of feature films for the big screen and TV, the most notable being David Lynch's *Fire Walk With Me* in 1992. She starred in the short-lived ABC series *To Have and to Hold* in 1998.

Character Bio:

Mandy Hampton only appeared in *The West Wing*'s rookie season, and even then, her appearances became less and less frequent. A one-time love interest of Josh Lyman, she had a taste for fast cars and was known as a shrewd political strategist and a no-nonsense negotiator.

What the actor says:

About her character: "She's a fighter in a difficult business and has a lot of strength." (NBC 1999 press kit)

Moira Kelly, initially billed as one of the show's stars for her role as Mandy Hampton, did not make it past The West Wing*'s first season.*

ANDREA RENAULT/GLOBE PHOTOS

What her character says:

About an anticipated political conflict with Josh: "I want you at your fighting weight for when I start bitch-slapping you around the Beltway." (Episode 1, "The Pilot")

CHAPTER SEVEN

EPISODE GUIDE:

Season One — September 1999 to May 2000

REGULAR CAST, SEASON ONE

Martin Sheen as President Josiah (Jed) Bartlet
Allison Janney as Press Secretary Claudia Jean (C.J.) Cregg
Moira Kelly as Political Consultant Madeline (Mandy) Hampton
Rob Lowe as Deputy Communications Director Sam Seaborn
Richard Schiff as Communications Director Toby Ziegler
John Spencer as Chief of Staff Leo McGarry
Bradley Whitford as Deputy Chief of Staff Joshua (Josh) Lyman

PRODUCTION STAFF, SEASON ONE

EXECUTIVE PRODUCERS: Aaron Sorkin, Thomas Schlamme, and John Wells

CO-EXECUTIVE PRODUCER: Michael Hissrich
PRODUCERS: Llewellyn Wells, Kristin Harms
DIRECTORS: Thomas Schlamme, Michael Lehmann, Marc Buckland, Anthony Drazan, Christopher Misiano, Alan Taylor, Bill D'Elia, Alex Graves, Kevin Rodney Sullivan, Arlene Sanford, Ken Olin, Clark Johnson, Laura Innes, Robert Berlinger, Don Scardino
CREATED BY: Aaron Sorkin
WRITERS: Aaron Sorkin, Lawrence O'Donnell Jr., Patrick Caddell, Paul Redford, Ron Osborn, Jeff Reno, Rick Cleveland, Dee Dee Myers
DIRECTOR OF PHOTOGRAPHY: Tom Del Ruth
CONSULTANTS: Patrick Caddell, Dee Dee Myers

EPISODE: 1

EPISODE TITLE: *Pilot*
ORIGINAL AIR DATE: Wednesday, September 22, 1999
WRITTEN BY: Aaron Sorkin, Lawrence O'Donnell Jr., and Patrick Caddell
DIRECTED BY: Thomas Schlamme
GUEST STARS: Annie Corley as Mary Marsh; F. William Parker as the Rev. Al Caldwell
ALSO STARRING: Lisa Edelstein as Laurie; Suzy Nakamura as Kathy; Allison Smith as Mallory; Janel Moloney as Donna; Kathryn Joosten as Mrs. Landingham; Devika Parikh as Bonnie
AWARDS:

> Jon Hutman (Productions Designer), Tony Fanning (Art Director), and Ellen Totleben (Set Decorator) won an Emmy for Outstanding Art Direction for a Single-Camera Series
>
> Thomas A. Del Ruth, A.S.C. (Director of Photography) won an Emmy for Outstanding Cinematography for a Single-Camera Series
>
> Thomas Schlamme (Director) won an Emmy for Outstanding Directing for a Drama Series

SUMMARY

We meet The West Wing*'s cast. The staff confronts the religious right, deals with a boatload of Cuban refugees, and Sam has a terrible day.*

The basic expectations for the pilot episode of any TV series are pretty simple — introduce the characters, set the tone and the pace of the show, and leave the audience wanting more. The opening installment of *The West Wing* accomplished all three.

Many critics believed that Sorkin used the pilot episode to parody Rob Lowe's lady-killer image (and his notorious sex-tapes scandal) to immediately put to rest the idea that the Sam character was only around because of his good looks and charm. It was accomplished in fine style in his unwitting liaison with Laurie, and the ridiculous White House tour he tries to conduct for a group of visiting school kids.

The pilot also established the show's pacing for episodes to come — continual switching back and forth between characters and sub-plots, with loads of the walk-and-talk scenes around the offices that would soon become a trademark of *The West Wing*. Folks who had enjoyed this kind of frenetic action on Sorkin's earlier series *Sports Night* recognized the pacing — those who hadn't quickly realized that this was going to be a show where viewers wouldn't be getting much of a mental break with everything that was going on.

The device Sorkin uses to introduce us to all the main characters was classic theater. Although we don't get to see POTUS until the final scene, we already know a fundamental truth about him — he is, as Leo says, a "bit of a klutz." What's the leader of the free world doing riding his bike into a tree? But Sheen makes his big entrance so powerfully, and denounces the visitors from the religious right with such power and eloquence, that we immediately realize that even if he is a little eccentric at times, it's an eccentricity leavened by a ton of conviction and strong will.

The other characters' habits and quirks are sketched out quickly — Leo's a hard-nosed perfectionist, Josh a workaholic, C.J. a bit of a bumbler and a good hearted romantic, Toby is dour and has little time for bureaucratic details, and Mandy is a take-no-prisoners strategist.

One final note: Sheen's "Lambs of God" speech to Mary Marsh and Al Caldwell has a basis in reality. In a press conference to launch the show, Sorkin admitted that he would be sending a few personal "soapbox" pronouncements through the characters in *The West Wing*, and used this device because he wanted to take a strip out of a real-life right-wing religious group.

EPISODE: 2

EPISODE TITLE: *Post Hoc, Ergo Propter Hoc* (some sources cite this as *Bartlet*)
ORIGINAL AIR DATE: Wednesday, September 29, 1999
WRITTEN BY: Aaron Sorkin
DIRECTED BY: Thomas Schlamme
GUEST STARS: Ruben Santiago Hudson as Morris Tolliver; Merrin Dungey as Daisy; John Bedford Lloyd as Senator Lloyd Russell
ALSO STARRING: Lisa Edelstein as Laurie; Suzy Nakamura as Kathy, Allison Smith as Mallory; Janel Moloney as Donna; Kathryn Joosten as Mrs. Landingham; Tim Matheson as Vice President John Hoynes; Renée Estevez as Nancy

SUMMARY
Sam still can't get over Laurie; VP Hoynes stirs up trouble; and Bartlet's newly-appointed personal physician is killed when his plane is shot down over the Middle East.

After President Bartlet's grand and powerful entrance late in the pilot episode, Sorkin and crew needed to develop his character more fully — and they did it in grand style in the second episode.

The device used was POTUS's rather quick hiring of an African-American

Navy doctor named Morris Tolliver as his personal physician. (The fact that Tolliver is black also deflected criticism there were too many white faces in positions of power in the pilot.) Based on his quick hiring of Tolliver, the audience was immediately able to figure out a few key things about Bartlet: he's impetuous; he takes a fast liking to the people he likes (and vice versa, as we see in later episodes); he's something of an equal-opportunity employer; and "fundamental values" like marriage and family count for him (at one point during their initial meeting, Tolliver shows Bartlet a picture of his wife and new baby).

The President, however, is no pushover — as we find out in his clash in this episode with VP John Hoynes. For all of his quirky good-naturedness in dealing with Tolliver, we quickly see that Bartlet can also be a hard-nosed politician bent on reminding anyone who would forget who's the boss in the White House.

But when the plane carrying Tolliver and his family to a teaching hospital in Jordan is shot down by Syria, we get a look at another side of Bartlet. Hauled out of bed at 4 a.m. to receive the bad news, *this* version of POTUS is ready almost to declare war on the Syrians — he's hot-tempered, impetuous, and ready to plunge the entire nation into war because of a personal loyalty.

Not every actor could pull off such a complex role, especially in an hour-long TV show, but Martin Sheen does. Even without the benefit of seeing his work in the following 42 episodes, the expansion of his character in this episode showed us this was one complex president, and one brilliant actor playing him.

EPISODE: 3

EPISODE TITLE: *A Proportional Response*
ORIGINAL AIR DATE: Wednesday, October 6, 1999
WRITTEN BY: Aaron Sorkin
DIRECTED BY: Marc Buckland

GUEST STARS: John Amos as Admiral Percy Fitzwallace; Merrin Dungey as Daisy; John Bedford Lloyd as Senator Lloyd Russell
ALSO STARRING: Lisa Edelstein as Laurie; Suzy Nakamura as Kathy; Allison Smith as Mallory; Janel Moloney as Donna; Kathryn Joosten as Mrs. Landingham; Tim Matheson as Vice President John Hoynes; Renée Estevez as Nancy; Devika Parikh as Bonnie; Nicole Robinson as Margaret

SUMMARY
An agitated Bartlet tries to figure out an appropriate military reaction to the Syrian attack in Episode 2; CJ is on the warpath for not being informed of Sam's dalliance with Laurie; and Josh hires a new personal aide for the president.

While the "proportional response" of the episode's title concerns Bartlet's quandary over how to retaliate against the Syrians, this one will go down in the history of *The West Wing* as The Episode Where Charlie Got Hired.

By including the young actor Dulé Hill in the cast as Bartlet's aide Charlie Young, Sorkin was able to accomplish two things: add an African-American presence to the show's core cast, and bring the superbly talented Hill into a key role.

Hill says that when he got the call to audition for the part, he had seen the pilot and wanted to be part of it, and put all his efforts into getting the role. After reading twice for Sorkin, Lewellyn Wells, and Tommy Schlamme, the part was his.

A recurring theme — that many of the characters do their jobs with equal parts patriotism and awe that they've actually been hired to serve president and country — comes through strongly when Josh Lyman is interviewing Charlie. Thinking he is being interviewed for a messenger's job, Charlie still can't quite believe he's actually in the White House. When it finally dawns on him that he's getting the position of personal aide to the President, he's stunned — but in an important sense, his amazement is something the entire staff feels daily.

There must have been considerable concern in Sorkin's mind that he was creating the role of a young black man who was essentially a modern-day manservant to a powerful white male. How well would it go over with the larger audience?

Craftily, Sorkin solved this problem by including a scene between Leo and Admiral Fitzwallace, who's also black. Leo asks the military man if he can imagine any problem with the Charlie hire. Admiral Fitzwallace assures Leo that as long as Charlie is being paid a respectable wage and treated like any other staffer, there should be no problems. ("I got some real honest-to-God battles to fight, Leo," Fitzwallace tells him. "I don't have time for the cosmetic ones.")

One final point about Charlie is worth noting within the larger picture of *The West Wing*'s cast: he's the only one of the core group who's actually *from* Washington, having grown up there the son of a police officer (his mother) and an absentee dad.

EPISODE: 4

EPISODE TITLE: *Five Votes Down*
ORIGINAL AIR DATE: Wednesday, October 13, 1999
WRITTEN BY: Aaron Sorkin (teleplay); Lawrence O'Donnell Jr. and Patrick Caddell (story)
DIRECTED BY: Michael Lehmann
GUEST STAR: Tim Matheson as Vice President John Hoynes
ALSO STARRING: Janel Moloney as Donna

SUMMARY
The staff have to lobby hard to reclaim five key votes on a weapons bill and it takes Hoynes's help to do it; Bartlet mixes meds and gets a little loopy; Leo's wife leaves him; and Toby is in danger of getting nailed for insider-trading.

A key episode for two reasons (three if you include seeing the President get wonky when he inadvertently combines back-pain medications). First, it allows the viewer some important insight into the character of Leo, and second, it further explores the tensions that exist between vp Hoynes, and Bartlet and his staff.

We've already seen Leo McGarry portrayed as a hard-driving perfectionist (in the pilot, he was visibly irked when the *New York Times* crossword misspelled "Khaddafi"), but basically a decent guy who was very loyal to his boss. In this episode, we actually get to see a few of his flaws, which brings up an interesting point about how we've come to regard most of the staff during the show's first two seasons. Based on the evidence, we can only conclude that these people have poured their entire being into their jobs. All they ever seem to do is work; we rarely get to see them at home or doing anything in their off-hours. Although there is the occasional mention of someone having gone on a date or attended a party, home or social life is almost never explored or even discussed (all of this excludes Bartlet, of course, whose attention to family life is a key aspect of the show).

At any rate, this episode marks a notable exception to this rule, since it includes the memorable event of Leo completely forgetting his anniversary, a gaffe that causes his wife Jenny to leave him. Leo doesn't help matters much by telling her that at this stage in his life, his job is more important to him than his marriage. Throughout the next 40 episodes, this statement essentially defines the Leo character — whatever feelings you might have for him, good or bad, whenever you see him in action, one is reminded of the incredible drive (maybe obsession) he brings to his job as White House Chief of Staff.

As Leo is also a recovering alcoholic and drug addict, this was the first of several times the question of whether a high-pressure situation would cause Leo to fall off the wagon was raised. As it turns out, he gets some surprising help from vp Hoynes — himself a recovering alcoholic — who invites him to a secret "card game" (actually an aa meeting). The goodwill gesture on Hoynes's part only complicates his character, because even though he's a good enough guy to extend a helping hand to Leo, he also shows himself to be a self-serving politico of the first order by playing hardball with Leo and the rest of the staff when they need his help to reclaim an errant Democrat vote on gun control. Hoynes gloats when he does it, telling the congressman he's reeled in that it might be a good idea to support him on this one because he will one day be president.

The episode concludes with one of its best vignettes to this point — Leo descending a dark staircase and telling a Secret Service agent at a door that he's there for the so-called "card game."

EPISODE: 5

EPISODE TITLE: *The Crackpots and These Women*
ORIGINAL AIR DATE: Wednesday, October 20, 1999
WRITTEN BY: Aaron Sorkin
DIRECTED BY: Anthony Drazan
GUEST STARS: Guy Boyd as Stanley; Janel Moloney as Donnatella Moss; Elisabeth Moss as Zoey Bartlet; Suzy Nakamura as Kathy; Renée Estevez as Nancy; Sam Lloyd as Bob; David Fabrizio as Jonathan Lacey
ALSO STARRING: Kathryn Joosten as Mrs. Landingham; Nicole Robinson as Margaret; Melissa Fitzgerald as Carol; Juwan Howard as Mr. Grant

SUMMARY
The staff plays an impromptu game of street basketball; the White House opens its doors to all kinds of zany visitors; Charlie and Zoey meet for the first time; and Mandy tells Toby he wasn't the first choice for the communications director job.

The opening game of pickup hoops sets the tone for the episode — generally light-hearted. Basketball fans will note that the "Mr. Grant" called in by Bartlet as a ringer for his side is, in real life, NBA star Juwan Howard, who then played for the Washington Wizards and now for the Dallas Mavericks. Bartlet's recruitment of the seven-footer reveals yet another aspect of his quirky character — someone who is not afraid to bend the rules a little in his favor. (Toby: "You know the thing about you, Mr. President, it isn't so much that you cheat, it's how brazenly bad you are at it.")

The word "crackpots" of the title refers to the fact that on the day in question, the White House (in apparent tribute to nineteenth-century prez Andrew Jackson, who used to do it all the time), opens its doors to any visitor who wants to drop by. Clearly, this was an attempt by Sorkin *et al* to establish the show as more than just week-in-week-out somber political drama. Josh Lyman calls the open-door policy "total crackpot day" and the same could be said for most of the episode. Indeed, during a time of pretty bleak prospects for the sitcom genre in general, *The West Wing* was beginning to emerge — and this installment went a long way to helping it in that direction — as one of the funnier shows in prime time.

In keeping with the general light tone of the episode, Bartlet announces to all that since his youngest daughter, Zoey, is coming to town for a visit, he is going to make chili for everyone — no questions asked. But the arrival of Zoey had far bigger implications for the show than just an excuse for a party. Not only did it introduce the character of Bartlet's youngest daughter (as played by Elisabeth Moss), it also marked the first meeting between her and Charlie Young, a growing relationship that would shape some major plotlines in the weeks to come.

EPISODE: 6

EPISODE TITLE: *Mr. Willis of Ohio*
ORIGINAL AIR DATE: Wednesday, November 3, 1999
WRITTEN BY: Aaron Sorkin
DIRECTED BY: Christopher Misiano
GUEST STARS: Al Fann as Joe Willis; Charley Lang as Congressman Skinner; Michael O'Neill as Ron Butterfield; Kenneth Tigar as Congressman Gladman
ALSO STARRING: Janel Moloney as Donna; Elisabeth Moss as Zoey; Allison Smith as Mallory; Suzy Nakamura as Kathy; Renée Estevez as Nancy

SUMMARY

*The husband of a deceased congresswoman has an impact on national politics;
and the Zoey/Charlie romance leads to a racial incident in a bar, which causes
Bartlet to seriously consider extra security for his daughter.*

More than a few critics have suggested that thanks to his work on *The
American President* and *A Few Good Men* (and *The West Wing*), Aaron Sorkin
is a kind of modern-day Frank Capra — a kind of gee-whiz patriot of the
cinematic variety.

That interpretation certainly got a boost in this episode. The "Mr. Willis"
in question is a slightly chubby black man who's an 8th-grade social studies
teacher and husband of a deceased Ohio congresswoman. He has come to DC
to vote on a bill concerning statistical sampling in the census (a process that
in a moment of unguarded honesty, C.J. and Sam agree they don't understand
at all). In addition to reminding audiences that the U.S. Constitution allows
the spouse of a dead member of Congress to vote on certain bills, the episode
invoked a classic Capra-esque motif: how a regular Joe can effect and affect
U.S. politics at the highest level (see Capra's 1939 classic *Mr. Smith Goes to
Washington* starring Jimmy Stewart).

Mr. Willis's insistence on discussing the census bill earnestly with the two
other congressmen with key votes, instead of quickly toeing the Democratic
party line, puts him in that Capra tradition of the small man who feels he has
to make big decisions in Washington. Capra wanted the Mr. Smith role to prod
moviegoers into taking a careful look at U.S. politics, instead of seeing it as
simply a monolithic machine. It appears Sorkin wanted to achieve the same
end in this episode. By having a "regular guy" figure interact with jaded professional politicians and staffers we're reminded that although the political
decision-making process comes across as slick and fast-paced on *The West
Wing*, the real-life and fictional decisions that are made at the White House
and in Congress still affect — and are affected by — the average person.

EPISODE: 7

EPISODE TITLE: *The State Dinner*
ORIGINAL AIR DATE: Wednesday, November 10, 1999
WRITTEN BY: Aaron Sorkin and Paul Redford
DIRECTED BY: Thomas Schlamme
GUEST STARS: Stockard Channing as Abigail Bartlet
ALSO STARRING: Lisa Edelstein as Laurie; Janel Moloney as Donna; Timothy Busfield as Danny; Kathryn Joosten as Mrs. Landingham; Melissa Fitzgerald as Carol; Ariono Suriawinata as President of Indonesia

SUMMARY

Staff members contend with a dour Indonesian president at a state dinner; Hurricane Sarah threatens the U.S. east coast; a hostage-taking occurs in Idaho; and teamsters are about to go on strike.

For those viewers who remember the basic high school lesson about the twofold responsibilities of the American president — to shape domestic policy and conduct foreign relations — this installment gives a good indication of how his staff assists Bartlet in conducting the latter task. Using the setting of a state dinner in honor of the visiting president of Indonesia, Sorkin and co-writer Paul Redford explored a number of different aspects of Bartlet's foreign-diplomacy approach, and in particular, how the messages he sends to the rest of the world are formulated by his staff.

For starters, there was the character of the Indonesian president to work around — here is a man of very few words, and less humor, and Bartlet confesses at one point that he could not imagine many people voting for him. But diplomacy is diplomacy, and that's illustrated by the fine line that Toby and Sam, as the official crafters of the words Bartlet speaks for the world to hear, have to walk as they work on a toast for Bartlet to make during the dinner. The speech-writing scenes illustrate a key aspect of Toby and Sam's jobs: they must continually keep in mind several audiences — and potential groups of voters or foreign allies — every time they put words on paper for Bartlet's public utterances. Throughout the series' first two seasons, they're constantly having to add or delete lines from speeches to reflect special-interest audiences.

In the state dinner speech, Toby and Sam have to strike a balance between welcoming their guest while not going overboard in praising a country with a dubious human-rights record. Officially, they want the U.S. to go on record as asking Indonesia to make good on the promises of the country's new constitution, but Toby has another motive. After the speech, he asks an Indonesian senior aide (with the improbable name of Bambang) to release from custody a friend of his who's been organizing anti-government protests. Just to prove you can't please all of the people all of the time, Bambang tells Toby that he has a lot of nerve writing a speech humiliating the Indonesian president and then asking for a favor.

EPISODE: 8

EPISODE TITLE: *Enemies*
ORIGINAL AIR DATE: Wednesday, November 17, 1999
WRITTEN BY: Ron Osborn and Jeff Reno (teleplay); Rick Cleveland, Lawrence O'Donnell Jr., and Patrick Caddell (story)
DIRECTED BY: Alan Taylor
GUEST STARS: Charley Lang as Congressman Skinner
ALSO STARRING: Timothy Busfield as Danny Concannon; Janel Moloney as Donna Moss; Allison Smith as Mallory O'Brien; Tim Matheson as John Hoynes; Renée Estevez as Nancy; Kathryn Joosten as Mrs. Landingham; Devika Parikh as Bonnie
AWARDS: Osborn, Reno, Cleveland, O'Donnell, and Caddell received a 2000 Writers Guild of America Award nomination for this episode.

SUMMARY

A series of one-on-one relationships are highlighted: Bartlet and Hoynes; Danny and C.J.; and Mallory and Sam (this one without Leo's blessing).

Typically, in any episode of *The West Wing*, there are so many interconnected plot lines and story arcs that there's little time for much serious one-on-one relationship development. This episode was a pleasant exception, but as its title suggests, not all of the pairings were friendly.

The first of the one-on-ones involves the Bartlet-Hoynes partnership at the top of the Democratic food chain. Bartlet still resents the fact that he needed a lot of help from Hoynes to win the presidential race, and the VP is taking every opportunity to remind him — and others — of his importance to the administration. The tension between the two has been brewing since Episode Two and will continue for some time. Of course, Bartlet is not about to let Hoynes push him around, and the two go at each other at a cabinet meeting, with Bartlet coming out on top and embarrassing Hoynes.

This provides a springboard for viewers to see C.J. doing her stuff, in this case trying her best to keep the Bartlet/Hoynes feud from the hitting the media. In turn, that allows us to see another important one-on-one relationship — one that will continue throughout season one — between *Washington Post* reporter Danny Concannon and C.J., who has to cut a deal with him to keep news of the spat from getting out. As Danny continues to pester C.J. for a date while they both struggle with the question of whether or not it's OK for a Press secretary to become involved with a member of the press corps (it's clear that the pair are attracted to each other) the mounting tension injects some excellent banter into the episode.

In the third pairing, Leo's daughter Mallory (who's aware of Sam's relationship with Laurie), asks Sam out to the opera, re-establishing the interaction started back in the pilot when Sam attempted the ill-fated White House tour for Mallory's grade-school class. In a bit of levity, Leo, who's no fan of the relationship, gives Sam a dumb assignment, writing a birthday message from the President to an assistant secretary of transportation, in an attempt to thwart his daughter's plans for the evening. Once again, we get to see the Sam character flounder a bit in matters of the heart — and another probable attempt by Sorkin to keep Rob Lowe from becoming too much of a sex symbol on the show.

EPISODE: 9

EPISODE TITLE: *The Short List*
ORIGINAL AIR DATE: Wednesday, November 24, 1999
WRITTEN BY: Aaron Sorkin and Patrick Caddell (teleplay), Aaron Sorkin and Dee Dee Myers (story)
DIRECTED BY: Bill D'Elia
GUEST STARS: Edward James Olmos as Roberto Mendoza; Holmes Osborne as "Congressman"; Mason Adams as Joseph Crouch; Ken Howard as Peyton Cabot Harrison
ALSO STARRING: Timothy Busfield as Danny Concannon; Janel Moloney as Donna

SUMMARY

Bartlet makes a decision to nominate a new Supreme Court judge to fill a vacancy caused by a retirement and almost immediately regrets his choice; a headline-seeking congressman alleges that one in three White House staffers use drugs, but the staff think he's really after Leo.

Sorkin and his team of writers take on a much-debated question during the past decade — drug use among employees. On *The West Wing*, the possibility of drug use among the president's staff has serious ramifications and that's exactly why a publicity-hungry congressman publicly charges that one in three White House staffers are drug users.

Given Sorkin's experiences with his own cocaine addiction, the episode marked an opportunity for him to develop, through Leo, a character who has overcome an addiction but continues to be vilified for it. Josh is the first to realize that the real target of the allegations is Leo, and prepares to defend his boss against a possible investigation into his past. The attitude he shares with his fellow staffers seems to be, "hey — the guy had a problem once, he's over it, now leave him alone." And that could very well have been Sorkin's rallying cry at that particular point in his career. He had two prime-time hits and a couple of solid movies under his belt; why then couldn't people just let the drug thing die for a while?

It's worth mentioning something here about substance abuse and *The West Wing* in general. Most viewers know that in real life, Martin Sheen is a recovering alcoholic who credits AA's 12-step plan with saving him. John Spencer is another admitted former drinker, and Rob Lowe has spoken on many occasions about how he sobered up and cut back on partying after his excesses during the late '80s. On the show, in addition to continual references to Leo's former drinking problem, we discover via a flashback in season two that Toby's career was at one point in trouble because of excessive boozing. Clearly, the high-pressure world of Washington politics — and, apparently of Hollywood TV and film-making — takes its toll on many creative personalities. Is it possible Sorkin is exorcising some of his personal demons through these characters and plotlines?

EPISODE: 10

EPISODE TITLE: *In Excelsis Deo*
ORIGINAL AIR DATE: Wednesday, December 15, 1999
WRITTEN BY: Aaron Sorkin
DIRECTED BY: Thomas Schlamme
ALSO STARRING: Lisa Edelstein as Laurie; Suzy Nakamura as Kathy; Allison Smith as Mallory; Janel Moloney as Donna; Kathryn Joosten as Mrs. Landingham; Devika Parikh as Bonnie; Kim Webster as Ginger; Renée Estevez as Nancy; Nicole Robinson as Margaret; Timothy Busfield as Danny

AWARDS:

Bill Johnson, A.C.E. (Editor) received an Emmy nomination for Outstanding Single-Camera Picture Editing for a Series.

Kenneth B. Ross (Production Mixer), Dan Hiland, Gary D. Rogers, and Len Schmitz (Production Mixers) received an Emmy nomination for Outstanding Sound Mixing for a Drama Series.

Aaron Sorkin and Rick Cleveland won an Emmy for Outstanding Writing for a Drama Series.

Sorkin and Cleveland were also nominated for a 2000 Writers Guild of America Award.

SUMMARY

Toby learns about the death of a homeless Korean War veteran and organizes his funeral; C.J. is enraged by the beating death of a gay high school senior; Josh and Sam work to keep the heat of a substance-abuse investigation off Leo.

One of the classic all-time *West Wing* episodes, as evidenced by the Emmy won by writers Sorkin and Cleveland for their script.

The main plot arc follows Toby, who learns about the death of a Korean War vet from exposure on a park bench. The death seems all the more tragic as Christmas approaches, and to add to the irony, the man happened to be wearing a coat that Toby had donated to charity. Toby takes it as a personal mission to organize an impressive funeral for the unfortunate vet.

This episode is all Richard Schiff, and was instrumental in winning him Best Supporting Actor Emmy for the season. One of the great things about Schiff's Toby Zeigler is that despite his hangdog expression and seemingly dour countenance, he can explode with emotion — anger and compassion being the two main ones — at perfectly-timed moments. Also, although Zeigler is an arch-strategist and political pragmatist par excellence, we get to see another side of his character that is anything but practical. On the highly-sentimental grounds that the vet who died was wearing his hand-me-down

Janney, Schiff and Moloney smooch it up at the 2000 Emmys

MILAN RYBA/GLOBE PHOTOS

coat, Toby goes all out to organize an elaborate funeral. When Bartlet tells him that such an event will mean that every homeless person in DC will come out of the woodwork looking for a similar handout, Toby doesn't care — he just wants to do what is right.

What clues does this episode give us as to the popularity of the Toby character? On more than a few previous occasions, and on many subsequent ones, he's proven himself to be downright abrasive, and lacks that crusty-but-lovable quality of Leo, and the imperious-but-quirky demeanor of Bartlet. Perhaps it's because many viewers are attracted to people who are completely dedicated to a cause. More than any other character on *The West Wing*, you get the sense that Toby can do nothing else but his job (in a later episode he admits that being a political strategist and communications wonk is all he ever does, and has ever done aside from attending Temple). Call it an "intangible," but whatever the case, in this episode, Toby emerges as the most determined and forthright character in the cast.

EPISODE: 11

EPISODE TITLE: *Lord John Marbury*
ORIGINAL AIR DATE: Wednesday, January 5, 2000
WRITTEN BY: Aaron Sorkin and Patrick Caddell (teleplay); Patrick Caddell and Lawrence O'Donnell Jr. (story)
DIRECTED BY: Kevin Rodney Sullivan
GUEST STARS: Roger Rees as Lord John Marbury; John Amos as Admiral Percy Fitzwallace; Iqbal Theba as the Ambassador from India
ALSO STARRING: Suzy Nakamura as Kathy; Janel Moloney as Donna; Kathryn Joosten as Mrs. Landingham; Elisabeth Moss as Zoey Bartlet; Nicole Robinson as Margaret; Devika Parikh as Bonnie; Melissa Fitzgerald as Carol

SUMMARY

British diplomat Lord John Marbury is recruited to try to resolve a border dispute between India and Pakistan; Leo detests him; Toby tells C.J. she is getting too friendly with the press; the investigation of Leo continues.

The "Lord John Marbury" of the episode's title is a roguish, hard-drinking, womanizing British diplomat who's brought in by Bartlet to act as a go-between in a border dispute that erupted when India invaded Pakistan territory in the Kashmir, and the threat of a nuclear war becomes very real. Marbury is played by Roger Rees, who TV fans recognized as the annoying corporate banker Robin Colcord from *Cheers*.

Leo finds Lord Marbury extremely annoying. For some reason — most likely the inevitable conflict between Leo's down-to-earth nature and Marbury's eccentric aristocratic airs — the two men take an almost immediate dislike to each other (Leo: "He thinks I'm the butler!"). But Marbury is an undisputed diplomatic expert, with ties to both India and Pakistan, so Bartlet argues for his inclusion in diplomatic talks.

Rees plays the part brilliantly — he captures Marbury's aristocratic arrogance without going over the top and turning him into some kind of parody of an in-bred Oxbridge diplomat. On several occasions, Rees seems half-crazed — it's obvious he's almost always a little tipsy and he always has an eye out for women — but manages to bring things under control, and to make the staffers realize that he actually does know what he's doing in matters diplomatic. Bartlet seems to respect him, although it's possible he might be playing devil's advocate just to irritate Leo.

John Spencer carries off the part of a resentful Leo perfectly — the Chief of Staff's salty charm comes across beautifully in his resentment of Marbury, especially since many of his lines are delivered not to the diplomat's face, but as complaints to the other staffers, who have their own run-ins with the Brit and find him equally off-putting. All of the Marbury/Leo tension builds within another subplot — the impending investigation into Leo's addictions and the possibility that his earlier sojourn in a rehab clinic would be entered into the court records.

EPISODE: 12

EPISODE TITLE: *He Shall, From Time to Time . . .*
ORIGINAL AIR DATE: Wednesday, January 12, 2000
WRITTEN BY: Aaron Sorkin
DIRECTED BY: Arlene Sanford
GUEST STARS: Roger Rees as Lord John Marbury; John Amos as Admiral Percy Fitzwallace
ALSO STARRING: Stockard Channing as Abigail Bartlet; Allison Smith as Mallory O'Brien; Timothy Busfield as Danny Concannon; Janel Moloney as Donna Moss

SUMMARY
Bartlet faints just before he has to give his first State of the Union address and it turns out he's suffering from more than just the flu; Lord Marbury settles the differences between India and Pakistan; Leo publicly announces his former

*battles with drugs and alcohol; Danny and C.J. exchange kisses, as do Mallory
and Sam.*

Until now, we'd seen many sides of President Bartlet — all of them pretty
positive. From Sorkin's dialogue, the President had been revealed as a man
with a diverse personality: intelligent, witty, well-read, decidedly eccentric,
loyal, hot-tempered, and kind. But in this episode — perhaps it wasn't coin-
cidence that this one marked the half-way point of the first season — we also
got to see another side of Bartlet: a man with physical weaknesses. Until now
he'd been shown to be a little clumsy, riding into a tree on his bike, and we
came to learn he'd been taking medication for back pain. But for someone in
his late-50s, Bartlet seemed in pretty good shape — certainly good enough to
play pickup basketball and golf from time to time.

In this episode, Bartlet's collapse before he was to give one of the most
important speeches of his political career was a major divergence, transforming him from a seemingly all-powerful, invincible leader to a man with
profound health problems (in this case, multiple sclerosis). Sheen plays the
aftermath of his collapse beautifully, as a typical older man who denies that
there is anything seriously wrong with him. When we learn his collapse is a
manifestation of his MS, ominous questions emerge: How will this affect his
presidency? What about his day-to-day life? Who else knows about his condition? Will he run for another term?

Of course, all of these questions would come cascading back toward the
end of season two — for now, the groundwork was just being laid. Oddly, the
Bartlet-MS subplot remained more or less buried for a long time afterwards
— more than a full season, when the issue rears up again in Episode 40. One
of the neat plot devices revolving around the Bartlet collapse is the reaction
of the other characters. Most notably, Toby barely seems to notice what has
happened; he's too wrapped up in the State of the Union speech he is fever-
ishly polishing for Bartlet. But the first Lady certainly does — as a highly-
qualified MD, we can expect her input on her husband's condition will matter
a lot in upcoming episodes.

EPISODE: 13

EPISODE TITLE: *Take Out the Trash Day*
ORIGINAL AIR DATE: Wednesday, January 26, 2000
WRITTEN BY: Aaron Sorkin
DIRECTED BY: Ken Olin
GUEST STARS: Dakin Matthews as Simon Bly; James Handy as
Congressman Bruno; Ray Baker as Mr. Lydell; Liza Weil as Karen Larson;
Linda Gehringer as Mrs. Lydell
ALSO STARRING: Timothy Busfield as Danny Concannon; Janel
Moloney as Donna; Suzy Nakamura as Kathy; Renée Estevez as Nancy

SUMMARY
*Josh and Sam make a bargain to keep Leo from going through a hearing on his
drug abuse; Mandy thinks that the family of the teen killed in a gay-bashing
should not attend the unveiling of an anti-hate-crimes law, while C.J. is mysti-
fied at why the boy's father is still ashamed of his dead son's homosexuality.*

An excellent episode for fans of C.J. Cregg. At this point in the series there
must have been many people, both at home and in Hollywood, who had
fallen in love with the character and the actress who plays her. In this installment, Janney got the chance to expand the C.J. character considerably, and
she really delivered.

The plot device that underpinned the episode began back in Episode 10
with the death of a gay high school student at the hands of a mob of homo-
phobic 13-year-olds in Minnesota. The incident sparked a move for
anti-hate-crime legislation, and by this point, the bill is ready to be signed.
The question is whether or not the young man's family should make the trip
to DC to witness the signing of the bill. Consultant Mandy Hampson thinks it
is a bad idea, while C.J. supports it. For the family's part, the father is still
embarrassed by his dead son's sexual preference, and that's what C.J. can't

figure out: how can a father continue to be ashamed at a trait in his son that ultimately led to his murder?

It's that mystification that brings out Janney's performance in this episode. Until now, we'd seen her character confront all kinds of high-pressure crises, while contending with a budding (and conscience-testing) relationship with reporter Danny Concannon. Janney had played those scenes with C.J.'s trademark sardonic wit and coolness under fire, although it became clear that the developing romance and its attendant ethical implications were beginning to gnaw at her. But all in all, she'd developed into a pretty savvy character, one you'd be happy to have on your side when the going got tough.

In the case of the family of the dead gay teen, we got to see C.J. confront an ethical issue she doesn't completely understand. As is often the case with Sorkin's writing, issues that at first seem cut-and-dried can sometimes become extremely murky, while the once assured character involved ends up realizing there might be another side to the story. Although C.J. can't comprehend the father's feelings, she realizes that he must have reasons for thinking the way he does, and that she can't entirely put herself in his shoes. It's that tension that makes for great drama — and for greatness in the C.J. character, and another reason Janney won an Emmy for her efforts.

For those who wonder if the show portrays Washington politics accurately, this episode is of particular interest. As an offshoot of the main plot, Leo initially fires an aide named Karen Larson for leaking information about his drug rehab to the press, and later, in a burst of compassion, decides to re-hire her. Sorkin reported later that he received a number of e-mails from White House staff saying that there was no way that this re-hiring would ever happen in real life — once fired, staffers stay fired!

EPISODE: 14

EPISODE TITLE: *Take This Sabbath Day*
ORIGINAL AIR DATE: Wednesday, February 9, 2000
WRITTEN BY: Aaron Sorkin, Paul Redford, and Lawrence O'Donnell Jr.
DIRECTED BY: Thomas Schlamme
GUEST STARS: Marlee Matlin as Joey Lucas; Karl Malden as Father John Cavanaugh; Noah Emmerich as Bobby Zane; Bill O'Brien as Kenny; David Proval as Rabbi Glassman; Felton Perry as Herb Mitchell
ALSO STARRING: Janel Moloney as Donna; Suzy Nakamura as Kathy; Renée Estevez as Nancy
AWARDS: Sorkin, Redford, and O'Donnell were nominated for a 2000 Writers Guild of America Award

SUMMARY

Bartlet has to decide whether or not to commute a death sentence and seeks advice from a priest; we meet Joey Lucas for the first time and she and Josh immediately clash.

Despite all that's been written since the time of Thomas Jefferson about the separation of church and state in American government, the Josiah Bartlet we've seen up until now has made no bones about showing his Catholicism. In fact, Bartlet's particular religious affiliation was something Martin Sheen insisted on before he accepted the role. Even though most American presidents have known the wisdom and necessity of separating church and state in the running of the country this does not prevent a highly moral leader like Bartlet from having his ethics shaped by his religious beliefs.

Those beliefs were put to the test in this installment, through the plot device of the President having to decide in less than 48 hours whether or not to commute the sentence of a man convicted of murdering a pair of drug lords. After the Supreme Court decides against a stay of execution, Bartlet must decide whether the murderer will live or die. Looking around desperately for guidance — he turns to his Catholic roots and consults Father Cavanaugh, his priest from boyhood. The priest is played by veteran actor Karl Malden, who adds just the right touch of piety to his advice for Bartlet. For those interested in how *The West Wing* reflects real life, it's worth noting that the stay-of-execution plot was based on an actual incident. In considering clemency for a convicted murderer named Jose Raul Garza, President Bill Clinton (unlike his fictional counterpart) decided to grant the stay.

At the same time, the religious side of another key character was also explored when Toby finds himself deeply conflicted over the impending execution, after hearing his rabbi speak about the evils of capital punishment. Although religion never plays a large part in plot development, it's always there in the background whenever these two characters are faced with moral or ethical decisions. And as viewers would see in episodes to come, Bartlet's Catholicism, first fleshed out and developed here, would loom large in his ethical dilemma over his medical condition.

We can't end a discussion of this episode without noting it marked the first appearance of a significant secondary character — political consultant and pollster Joey Lucas, who, like Oscar-winner Marlee Matlin who plays her, is deaf. Her first task is to appeal to a skeptical Josh that the Democratic congressional candidate she's working for isn't getting adequate campaign funding. They get into a major argument, even though Lucas has to rely on her sign-language interpreter, Kenny, at times — it ends up in a draw. Two things are immediately apparent: an attractive and dynamic character like Lucas will be back in future episodes, and that Josh is most impressed with his adversary, and not just as a political foe, which sets the tone for later episodes when a Josh-Joey romance becomes a possibility.

EPISODE: 15

EPISODE TITLE: *Celestial Navigation*
ORIGINAL AIR DATE: Wednesday, February 16, 2000
WRITTEN BY: Aaron Sorkin, Dee Dee Myers, and Lawrence O'Donnell Jr.
DIRECTED BY: Christopher Misiano
GUEST STARS: CCH Pounder as Deborah O'Leary; Robert David Hall as Nessler; Vaughan Armstrong as McNamara
ALSO STARRING: Timothy Busfield as Danny Concannon; Janel Moloney as Donna; Edward James Olmos as Roberto Mendoza

SUMMARY
Josh goes to a local college for a lecture on life at the White House; Bartlet's nominee for the Supreme Court is arrested and detained and Sam and Toby must bail him out.

In a departure from the sequential unfolding of events that has characterized *The West Wing* to this point, Sorkin makes use of extensive flashbacks in this episode. Josh's guest lecture at a local college on White House politics and procedure is used as a jumping-off point, and while Josh is speaking, a number of stories and subplots fade in and out.

The mechanism used for the cut-aways is Josh's cell phone. As he is delivering his address to the college audience, he is continually interrupted by calls from Sam and Toby, who are keeping him abreast of their attempts to find the small Connecticut town where Roberto Mendoza, Bartlet's nominee for the Supreme Court, is sitting in a cell after being arrested for driving while under the influence.

Mendoza is superbly played by guest star Edward James Olmos, who many will remember from his role on *Miami Vice* and from his star turn as the teacher in the 1988 film *Stand and Deliver*. Part of the Mendoza dynamic in this episode hinges on his humiliation at being arrested while driving with his family; at one point he deadpans that "America just got another pissed-off guy with brown skin."

Toby and Sam's inability to find Mendoza, and Josh's inability to locate them in turn, emphasize a curious aspect of many of *The West Wing*'s staffers — on many occasions, they seem more like the Keystone Cops than savvy political operators. Ask them to develop important policy affecting the lives of millions and they can do it, with brilliance, but they appear incapable of reading a map. Toby and Sam getting lost isn't the only instance when characters on the show prove to be slightly inept at everyday things — Bartlet seems almost proud of his inability to learn how his intercom works, and Josh Lyman is forever having computer problems, to cite just two examples. To drive the point home even further, Sorkin even has Sam launch into one of his windy discourses about the U.S. road system — even though he appears incapable of finding his way around a tiny part of it.

Cinematically, the trick of wrapping the hour around Josh's speech and then jumping around works nicely, not just as a way of interspersing the Toby/Sam/Mendoza plot, but also as a way of working in several sub-plots. One of them involves veteran actress CCH Pounder in the role of Cabinet Secretary of Housing and Urban Development, Deborah O'Leary, who accuses a Republican congressman of being a racist, and another features scenes of Josh's disastrous attempt to work a press conference in the absence of C.J., who develops a major tooth abscess.

EPISODE: 16

EPISODE TITLE: *20 Hours in L.A.*
ORIGINAL AIR DATE: Wednesday, February 23, 2000
WRITTEN BY: Aaron Sorkin
DIRECTED BY: Alan Taylor
GUEST STARS: David Hasselhoff as himself; Jay Leno as himself;

Veronica Webb as herself; Marlee Matlin as Joey Lucas; Bob Balaban as Theodore "Ted" Marcus; Tim Matheson as Vice President John Hoynes **ALSO STARRING**: Jorja Fox as Gina Toscano; Janel Moloney as Donnatella Moss; Elisabeth Moss as Zoey Bartlet; John De Lancie as Al Kiefer; Bill O'Brien as Kenny; Michael O'Neill as Ron Butterfield; Nicole Robinson as Margaret

SUMMARY:

Most of the staff travels to L.A. for a Hollywood fundraiser; Josh tangles with a movie mogul over a proposed bill banning gays in the military; Zoey gets a new bodyguard; a possible romance builds between Josh and Joey; and Leo has to stay home to persuade Hoynes to break a tie in the Senate over an ethanol bill.

Most of the action in this episode takes place in California, as the gang heads out to Hollywood for a Democratic party fundraising event that features cameo appearances by Jay Leno, Veronica Webb, and David Hasselhoff, as themselves. Temporarily moving the action to L.A. was a nifty move by Sorkin *et al*, as it broke up the potential monotony of setting everything in DC. It also allowed many famous names to make appearances, which gave it a flavor of real-life conventions where the cinematically famous rub elbows with the politically powerful.

The focus of all the attention is movie mogul Ted Marcus, played by film and TV veteran Bob Balaban. Balaban achieved temporary TV fame in a run of *Seinfeld* episodes where Jerry and the gang are trying to make a series based on their lives. Balaban played the NBC exec who falls for Elaine and in an attempt to prove his is worthy of her, leaves the world of high-powered TV decision-making (which puts the kibosh on Jerry's show) to join a Greenpeace anti-whaling crew.

At any rate, Ted Marcus is all for organizing the big fundraiser — and adding the $2.5 million it expects to raise for the Democratic coffers — as long as Bartlet goes public with his opposition to a new bill banning gays in the military. At first, Marcus (who is gay) is set to take down all the party tents and cancel the catering, when Josh tells him that although Bartlet opposes the bill, he's not yet in a position to denounce it publicly. In a private meeting, Bartlet, who calls himself a "human starting pistol," tells Marcus that speaking out against the bill will only give it unnecessary attention, and that it's a bill with no future — which Marcus reluctantly accepts. The Marcus character is an excellent one — he knows that in dealing with Josh, he is not speaking to the man in charge, and treats him accordingly — and both he and Josh are aware that one word from Marcus and the Democrats are out some big bucks. It's not known whether Sorkin based the character on someone he'd dealt with before, but Marcus displays all the earmarks of the archetypal Hollywood producer: arrogant, witty, convinced he's right, and ultimately has a bit of conscience or soul.

Despite the fact that most of the good stuff is happening on the West Coast, one staffer who does not make the trip is Leo — he remains in Washington to persuade VP Hoynes that he needs to work to break a tie in the Senate on ethanol taxation. Their confrontation illustrates yet another one of the Hoynes-vs.-Bartlet-and-staff conflicts that pop up throughout the first two seasons, and once again establishes Leo as an ace political operative.

In the romance department, Josh finally musters up the courage to pay a visit to Joey, but when she answers the door in nothing but a towel, it's apparent she has a visitor — an irritating pollster named Al Kiefer. Viewers who always felt that for all his charm, Josh was someone who needed to be taken down a notch or two, would have enjoyed watching his reaction when he realizes that Joey isn't alone.

The episode also marked the introduction of a new character, Secret Service agent Gina Toscano, played by actress Jorja Fox. As seen in prior episodes, the romance between Zoey Bartlet and Charlie Young was generating some fairly negative attention; Toscano (as Zoey's bodyguard) is now on the scene to make sure the growing backlash doesn't escalate into something ugly.

EPISODE: 17

EPISODE TITLE: *The White House Pro-Am*
ORIGINAL AIR DATE: Wednesday, March 22, 2000
WRITTEN BY: Aaron Sorkin, Lawrence O'Donnell Jr., and Paul Redford
DIRECTED BY: Ken Olin
GUEST STARS: Stockard Channing as Abigail Bartlet; Amy Aquino as Congresswoman Becky Reisman; Nadia Dajani as Lily Mays
ALSO STARRING: Jorja Fox as Gina Toscano; Janel Moloney as Donnatella Moss; Elisabeth Moss as Zoey Bartlet; Timothy Busfield as Danny Concannon

SUMMARY

A group of white supremacists send death threats to the White House, angered at the Zoey/Charlie romance; Abby Bartlet airs her views on child labor in other countries, causing trouble for one of her husband's tariff bills and increases the marital tension by publicly endorsing an ex-boyfriend for a Treasury post.

"We don't handle my wife. When we try, you know what happens at the other end of this building?" Bartlet asks C.J. Cregg rhetorically in this episode. "I get a little punishment."

Although we'd seen Dr. Abigail Bartlet — better known as Abby — several times before, it was in this episode that we really found out what she was made of. It's clear that Sorkin didn't want Abby's character to develop as a woman whose main accomplishment in life was being married to the President. As an accomplished MD, she'd forged a highly-specialized and impressive career in medicine alongside her husband's in political career. And it became clear in this episode that she'd formed some solid opinions about matters of domestic and foreign policy — opinions she was not afraid to air publicly, regardless of who her husband happened to be.

The West Wing's creative team couldn't have found an actor more suitable to play Abby Bartlet than Stockard Channing. Although the veteran actress was initially surprised to be asked to take the role, she quickly put her imprint on it, establishing the First Lady as a no-nonsense soulmate and advisor to the President, and, perhaps most importantly, the one person who will never back down from Jed Bartlet, even when his dander's up.

When Dr. Bartlet goes public on a TV talk show with her views on child labor in other countries, her statements cause a female member of Congress to propose an amendment to an international tariff bill that the President has been pushing for a long time. Then, on the death of the chair of the Federal Reserve, the First Lady lets it be known that she favors the Reserve's second-in-command for the job — someone she used to date in college. The President's staff is up in arms about the comments, but Bartlet knows better. Indeed, this episode marked not only an expansion of the Abby Bartlet character, but went a long way in explaining the relationship between the President and First Lady — and it set the groundwork for similar clashes in future episodes.

Stockard Channing brings a veteran actor's poise to the role of the First Lady, Dr. Abigail Bartlet

RON DAVIS/SHOOTING STAR

EPISODE: 18

EPISODE TITLE: *Six Meetings Before Lunch*
ORIGINAL AIR DATE: Wednesday, April 5, 2000
WRITTEN BY: Aaron Sorkin
DIRECTED BY: Clark Johnson
GUEST STARS: Carl Lumbly as Jeff Breckenridge
ALSO STARRING: Jorja Fox as Gina Toscano; Janel Moloney as Donnatella Moss; Elisabeth Moss as Zoey Bartlet; Timothy Busfield as Danny Concannon; Suzy Nakamura as Kathy; Allison Smith as Mallory O'Brien; Lindsay Sloane as Stacy; Nicole Robinson as Margaret; Kim Webster as Ginger; Devika Parikh as Bonnie; Melissa Fitzgerald as Carol

SUMMARY

Josh confronts a congressman who's making noise about slave reparations; Mendoza is finally confirmed for the Supreme Court; Mandy pesters Toby for help in replacing a dead panda bear; Sam and Mallory argue about school vouchers.

The summer before *The West Wing*'s pilot episode hit the air in September, 1999, Moira Kelly was one of the cast members that NBC and Warner Brothers were promoting as a star of the new series. By the end of the first season, it was clear that Kelly would not be returning to the show.

No one is exactly sure what happened, or if they are, they're only saying in veiled terms — as Aaron Sorkin did near the end of the show's rookie season — that it was tough to give every actor in the show's ensemble cast as big a part as they might have wanted. Viewers following the progress of Kelly's character throughout the early episodes might have noticed she was appearing less frequently and more marginally. In this episode, past the three-quarter mark of the season, it was becoming clear that the Mandy character was on the way out. Her major role was to ask Toby — whom she'd insulted on more than a few occasions — to help her to replace a panda that had died at the National Zoo.

Perceptive fans watching *Six Meetings Before Lunch* might have concluded that if one of the main characters in the show when it launched seven months prior was now reduced to quibbling with a senior staffer over a dead panda, it's unlikely that character would survive past the first season.

Kelly always played her character — rumored widely to be based on the real-life Clinton strategist Mandy Grunwald — as a straight-ahead, no-nonsense veteran of the strategy wars. From the beginning, she'd let Josh (the two had a prior romantic history) know that she was not going to make life easy for him and the Bartlet administration because she worked for Senator Lloyd Russell in his bid for the presidency. When Russell dropped out of contention, Hampson was hired by Bartlet — much to Josh's dismay — and continued to make life tough for the West Wingers. She took on the task of trying to resolve the Idaho raid back in episode 7 (*The State Dinner*) but that ended disastrously, and although Mandy didn't seem to have lost her edge, it did seem that her character was given less to do in subsequent weeks.

Although *Six Meetings Before Lunch* is significant because it was the episode in which Judge Mendoza finally gets his seat on the Supreme Court after much tribulation and controversy, it will also go down in the minds of many fans as the beginning of the end of the Mandy character.

EPISODE: 19

EPISODE TITLE: *Let Bartlet Be Bartlet*
ORIGINAL AIR DATE: Wednesday, April 26, 2000
WRITTEN BY: Aaron Sorkin, Peter Parnell, and Patrick Caddell
DIRECTED BY: Laura Innes
GUEST STARS: John Amos as Admiral Percy Fitzwallace
ALSO STARRING: Timothy Busfield as Danny Concannon; Janel Maloney as Donna; Renée Estevez as Nancy

SUMMARY

The staff scramble to find out who wrote a memo that's circulating and is highly critical of Bartlet and his team and end up more motivated than ever; Josh tries some insider moves to get a pair of Democrats named to the Federal Exchange Commission; and Sam investigates the military's policy regarding gay members.

The staff is shocked to learn about a memo going around Washington that's highly critical of the Bartlet team, and suggests how political foes could take advantage of the team's vulnerabilities. The group tries to try to figure out who wrote it, and who has it. It turns out the author is none other than Mandy, who penned the memo while working for Lloyd Russell. Once everything is revealed, the team responds by agreeing on a new strategy — the "let Bartlet be Bartlet" of the episode's title, an assertion that the President's quirky ways are actually a source of political strength.

The episode also went a very long way toward establishing, or perhaps re-establishing the team that would carry the Bartlet agenda forward. Not coincidentally, the revelation that the memo had been written by Mandy also reinforced the fact that Moira Kelly wouldn't be returning after the first season.

Another character who ended up much less visible in season two was *Washington Post* reporter Danny Concannon. Just as the infamous memo appeared to doom the Mandy character, the plot device of having Danny break the story — and the memo — to the *Post* came to be seen as the thin edge of the wedge for the gradual reduction of the Concannon character in the series. Indeed, by the following episode, the newly-rejuvenated Bartlet team had all but ostracized both Mandy and Danny.

EPISODE: 20

EPISODE TITLE: *Mandatory Minimums*
ORIGINAL AIR DATE: Wednesday, May 3, 2000
WRITTEN BY: Aaron Sorkin

DIRECTED BY: Robert Berlinger
GUEST STARS: Marlee Matlin as Joey Lucas
ALSO STARRING: Timothy Busfield as Danny Concannon; Janel Maloney as Donna; John De Lancie as Al Kiefer; Suzy Nakamura as Kathy; Bill O'Brien as Kenny; Kathryn Joosten as Mrs. Landingham; Nicole Robinson as Margaret; Melissa Fitzgerald as Carol; Kim Webster as Ginger; Devika Parikh as Bonnie

SUMMARY

Team Bartlet is fired up in the aftermath of the Mandy memo and works to develop a new drug policy; Bartlet makes a big noise about his nominations to the Federal Elections Commission; Toby's ex enters the scene for a brief appearance; Joey Lucas returns.

One of the best things about *The West Wing* is the way the Sorkin team can take an arcane piece of American government legislation or policy and build an entire episode around it. Indeed, many viewers like the show because they feel there is actually some educational value in it. Sorkin has always resisted the "ripped from the headlines" approach to writing, but he isn't adverse to basing many episodes on real life events in Washington. Although Sorkin has maintained that a primetime TV show is not the proper vehicle for teaching civics lessons, his occasional forays into this territory does make for some pretty interesting drama.

In this episode, following up on a sub-plot that had been brewing for a few episodes, Bartlet finally makes his nominations to the Federal Elections Commission — amidst much controversy. Obviously, a plot built around a conflict in the Middle East or capital punishment could be counted on to attract huge audience interest. But the FEC? It's a good bet not very many Americans are overly familiar with the body, and Canadians even less so. By weaving the usual excellent dialogue around the struggle to nominate members — Josh is particularly vociferous about putting Democrats on the Commission — Sorkin encapsulates one of the key rules of watching *The*

West Wing: It doesn't really matter if you know what they are talking about politically; you just have to trust that it's all more or less accurate and follow the dialogue and drama and evaluate it on those grounds.

EPISODE: 21

EPISODE TITLE: *Lies, Damn Lies and Statistics*
ORIGINAL AIR DATE: Wednesday, May 10, 2000
WRITTEN BY: Aaron Sorkin
DIRECTED BY: Don Scardino
GUEST STARS: Marlee Matlin as Joey Lucas
ALSO STARRING: Lisa Edelstein as Laurie; Timothy Busfield as Danny Concannon; Thom Gossom Jr. as Ted Mitchell; David Huddleston as Max Lobell; Janel Moloney as Donnatella Moss; Austin Pendleton as Barry Haskell; Lawrence Pressman as Ken Cochran; Reiko Aylesworth as Janine; Renée Estevez as Nancy; Bill O'Brien as Kenny; Nicole Robinson as Margaret; Devika Parikh as Bonnie; Kim Webster as Ginger; Kris Murphy as Katie; Melissa Fitzgerald as Carol

SUMMARY
Bartlet does some political fancy footwork in the area of campaign finance; Sam shows he still has feelings for Laurie; C.J. is under pressure to prove she's not slipping in her job performance; a new poll looks good for Bartlet.

In a bizarre kind of way, the unifying theme in this episode is love, or at least a variation of it.

Nothing much had been heard about the Sam-Laurie relationship for a while, but in this episode, that sub-plot makes a resounding return. Although Sam realizes it would be career suicide to go to Laurie's graduation from law school, he still wants to give her a present, so he arranges a rendezvous. On an early show, Sam's old friend Josh accused him of having a lost-puppy affliction

— Sam's sentimental side cannot resist helping people who need it. Problem is, a photographer from a British tabloid sees them together, and captures their gift exchange on film. The resulting bad press infuriates Sam's superiors. (Bartlet to Sam, sarcastically: "It's nice when you can do something for prostitutes once in a while, isn't it?") Ultimately, Toby, Leo, and Bartlet end up supporting Sam, proving once again that on *The West Wing*, loyalty still rules.

But Bartlet is also having problems with amorously-inclined members of his government — he's forced to recall the U.S. ambassador to Bulgaria, who is carrying on an extra-marital affair with the daughter of the country's president. Oddly, the ambassador thinks Bartlet is recalling him because he'd insulted Charlie Young some years before when the presidential aide was a waiter at a Washington private club. What the ambassador didn't know was that Charlie never mentioned the run-in to the President. The controversy augurs poorly for Bartlet, as he awaits numbers from a poll assessing his popularity.

Meanwhile, C.J. is starting to think that she's failing in her duties as Press Secretary. Perhaps there was something to Toby's accusation back in Episode 11 that she was getting a little too soft on members of the press, and one bearded one in particular. Luckily for C.J., the presidential polling numbers are higher than she thought they'd be. And Josh continues his repartee with Joey Lucas — it is becoming more and more obvious that Josh is falling for the pollster, but it's unclear whether the growing attraction is mutual.

EPISODE: 22 (SEASON ONE FINALE)

EPISODE TITLE: *What Kind of Day Has It Been?*
ORIGINAL AIR DATE: Wednesday, May 17, 2000
WRITTEN BY: Aaron Sorkin
DIRECTED BY: Thomas Schlamme
GUEST STARS: John Amos as Admiral Percy Fitzwallace
ALSO STARRING: Tim Matheson as Vice President John Hoynes;

Timothy Busfield as Danny Concannon; Jorja Fox as Gina Toscano; Janel
Moloney as Donnatella Moss; Elisabeth Moss as Zoey Bartlet; Suzy
Nakamura as Kathy; Michael O'Neill as Ron Butterfield; Kathryn Joosten as
Mrs. Landingham; Nicole Robinson as Margaret; Melissa Fitzgerald as
Carol; Devika Parikh as Bonnie; Kim Webster as Ginger
AWARDS: Tina Hirsch, A.C.E. (Editor) was nominated for an Emmy for
Outstanding Single-Camera Picture Editing for a Series

SUMMARY
*Bartlet and staff deal with the aftermath when an American plane is shot down
over Iraq; Toby's brother is aboard a space shuttle that's having technical problems; and the President attends a "town hall meeting" with unforeseen and very
serious consequences.*

Wow! That's probably the best description of the final episode of *The West
Wing*'s rookie year. Even people who didn't follow the show soon found out
what happened — the episode's concluding scene, and the summer of
suspense that followed, made headlines across North America.

Among critics and many fans, though, the season-one finale was something of a mixed bag. Some people felt that the cliffhanger ending that would
keep people guessing over the summer was both an excellent piece of cinema
(the episode's camera work and editing was nominated for an Emmy Award)
and a great promotional technique for boosting ratings. Others thought that
leaving people hanging over the summer was little more than a cheap trick.
Even Sorkin, when discussing how he was planning to end the second season,
a year later, alluded to the fact that the season-one finale might have been a
little contrived in its attempts to manufacture some easy drama and a summer
of suspense.

Perhaps a better question than "what did you think of the ending?" would
be "did you see that particular ending coming?" Unlike its *Dallas* predecessor,
the unknown element in this episode was not who did the shooting, but who
was shot. Given the tension that had been building since the Zoey-Charlie

relationship began creating controversy back in Episode 6 and continuing with death threats and the hiring of Zoey's own bodyguard, it was ominously clear that something bad was going to happen — and soon.

One of the hallmarks of the episode — leaving aside the cliffhanger debate — was the masterful way Sorkin *et al* paced the action. In typical fashion, there was lots to grab and keep viewer interest for most of the hour, so that when the whole town hall sequence did erupt, it seemed to come out of the blue. Putting it another way, the sub-plots about Toby's brother aboard the faulty space shuttle and the controversy over the Iraqi shooting of the U.S. plane effectively diverted viewers from the fact that something big was going to happen at the town hall meeting, something that appeared to be just a low-key appearance for the president. When it did come, the sequence — easily the most important event on the show since it began — had the unexpected impact of a chain reaction car crash. It was almost as though Sorkin and his team decided to run it through quickly for maximum impact and effect after creating a series of unconnected sub-plots during the episode.

Whatever the case, and no matter what one may think about the techniques Sorkin used, the final scene did get people talking throughout the summer of 2000 and up until the new season began in October.

CHAPTER EIGHT

EPISODE GUIDE:

Season Two — October 2000 to May 2001

REGULAR CAST

Martin Sheen as President Josiah (Jed) Bartlet

Dulé Hill as Personal Aide Charlie Young

Allison Janney as Press Secretary Claudia Jean (C.J.) Cregg

Rob Lowe as Deputy Communications Director Sam Seaborn

Janel Moloney as Josh's Secretary, Donnatella (Donna) Moss

Richard Schiff as Communications Director Toby Ziegler

John Spencer as Chief of Staff Leo McGarry

Bradley Whitford as Deputy Chief of Staff Joshua (Josh) Lyman

PRODUCTION STAFF

EXECUTIVE PRODUCERS: Aaron Sorkin, Thomas Schlamme, and John Wells
CO-EXECUTIVE PRODUCER: Kevin Falls
PRODUCERS: Llewellyn Wells, Kristin Harms, Michael Hissrich, Lawrence O'Donnell Jr.
DIRECTORS: Thomas Schlamme, Alex Graves, Ken Olin, Christopher Misiano, Jeremy Kagan, Paris Barclay, Laura Innes, Scott Winant, Lou Antonio, Michael Engler, Jessica Yu, Bryan Gordon, Bill Johnson
CREATED BY: Aaron Sorkin
WRITERS: Aaron Sorkin, Peter Parnell, Allison Abner, Kevin Falls, Laura Glasser, Lawrence O'Donnell Jr., Paul Redford, Patrick H. Caddell, Dee Dee Myers, Pete McCabe, Felicia Willson
DIRECTOR OF PHOTOGRAPHY: Tom Del Ruth
CONSULTANTS: Dee Dee Myers, Marlin Fitzwater, Peggy Noonan
MUSIC OMPOSER: W.G. Snuffy Walden

EPISODE: 23

EPISODE TITLE: *In the Shadow of Two Gunmen* (part 1)
ORIGINAL AIR DATE: Wednesday, October 4, 2000
WRITTEN BY: Aaron Sorkin
DIRECTED BY: Thomas Schlamme
ALSO STARRING: Stockard Channing as Abby; Timothy Busfield as Danny; Tim Matheson as Vice President Hoynes; Elisabeth Moss as Zoey Bartlet; Michael O'Neill as Ron Butterfield; Nicole Robinson as Margaret; Jorja Fox as Gina Toscano; Anna Deveare Smith as National Security Adviser Nancy McNally; Melissa Fitzgerald as Carol; Kim Webster as Ginger; Kathryn Joosten as Mrs. Landingham

SUMMARY

The staff wait to see who's been hurt — and how badly — in the aftermath of the shooting that ended season one; through a series of flashbacks we see how Josh, Sam, and Toby first started working with Bartlet; the press pesters C.J. and Toby on why the president was left unprotected and who is in charge in his absence.

This episode aired back-to-back with number 24 on the first night of the show's 2000–2001 season. Although the main action centered around the injuries suffered by some of the staff, and the legal implications of having a president temporarily out of action, the really interesting thing about the two parts of *In the Shadow of Two Gunmen* was the fact that Sorkin *et al* decided to use these episodes to shed some light on the personal histories of the main characters; where they came from and how they ended up working for the Bartlet campaign and eventually the presidential administration.

One wonders why *The West Wing's* writing team waited this long and chose this episode to indulge in character biographies. It seems to have worked, as the new information viewers learned about Josh, Sam, and Toby in this episode (and C.J. and Donna in the next) certainly helped to explain what made these characters tick during the first season. It might have made more sense to get these background "explanations" out of the way earlier, but it's hard to argue with Sorkin's sense of dramatic timing, especially when it works as well as it does in Episodes 23 and 24. The explanatory flashbacks also brought up the interesting possibility that they might be used again — and were with equal effect in the season two finale.

EPISODE: 24

EPISODE TITLE: *In the Shadow of Two Gunmen* (part 2)
ORIGINAL AIR DATE: Wednesday, October 4, 2000
WRITTEN BY: Aaron Sorkin
ALSO STARRING: Stockard Channing as Abby; Timothy Busfield as

Danny; Elisabeth Moss as Zoey Bartlet; Michael O'Neill as Ron Butterfield; Nicole Robinson as Margaret; Melissa Fitzgerald as Carol

SUMMARY

Through more flashbacks, we see how Donna and C.J. first joined the Bartlet team; it is revealed that the shooters — now all in custody — were white supremacists gunning for Charlie; Josh suffers the most severe injuries and is still recovering.

Is it possible that the character of Donna is just a wee bit absurd? Make no mistake — the addition of Janel Moloney to the main cast for this second season was overdue, and her constant and possibly-romantically-motivated banter with Josh has provided excellent and much-needed moments of levity. But in this case, the flashback to Donna's first days as Josh's assistant only serve to make the character even less believable.

For example, there's the fact that she supposedly waltzed into the White House and "hired" herself as Josh's assistant, and had the brass to engage a top-ranking government official in snappy repartee. There's that gosh-I-just-want-to-serve-my-country quality that is kind of appealing in Rob Lowe's Sam that just doesn't ring as true for her. This episode also provided more clues about the budding (if still speculative) Josh–Donna romance by giving viewers a look at their early interaction, but Lyman is not exactly smitten with Donna at this point.

The way the C.J. flashback is handled — complete with her falling into a pool, thus establishing her klutzy reputation early on — is far more believable. It's no stretch of the imagination when you see her in her old job as a movie-studio promo flack, and one could easily imagine C.J. moving effortlessly from the one job to the other; while it's hard to imagine Donna just appearing at Josh's elbow without any credenitals or I.D. — and being allowed to stay.

EPISODE: 25

EPISODE TITLE: *The Midterms*
ORIGINAL AIR DATE: Wednesday, October 18, 2000
WRITTEN BY: Aaron Sorkin, Lawrence O'Donnell Jr., and Patrick Caddell
DIRECTED BY: Alex Graves
GUEST STARS: Claire Yarlett as Dr. Jenna Jacobs
ALSO STARRING: Elisabeth Moss as Zoey Bartlet; Nicole Robinson as Margaret; Melissa Fitzgerald as Carol; Devika Parikh as Bonnie; Kim Webster as Ginger

SUMMARY

Bartlet can't ignore a former rival in New Hampshire who's running for a school board position; Toby is determined to find a way to legislate against hate groups; the staff realize they have only three months left to win seats in Congress before mid-term elections; and Bartlet has a run-in with a radio show host.

Without question, the highlight of the episode was Bartlet's encounter with Dr. Jenna Jacobs, a thinly-disguised fictional version of Dr. Laura Schlessinger, the popular nationally syndicated radio host who'd been making headlines for her vocal and Bible-based opposition to homosexuality.

Bartlet's verbal attack on Dr. Jacobs seems to have been inspired by an open letter to Laura Schlessinger that was floating around the Internet, in which an unsigned wag asked the radio host about certain injunctions against behavior as specified by scripture. For example, "I would like to sell my daughter into slavery as sanctioned in Exodus 21:7. In this day and age, what do you think would be a fair price for her?" or "I know from Lev. 11:6–8 that touching the skin of a dead pig makes me unclean, but may I still play football if I wear gloves?" or "Lev. 21:20 states that I may not approach the altar of God if I have a defect in my sight. I have to admit that I wear reading glasses. Does my vision have to be 20/20 or is there some flexibility here?"

Bartlet cites several of these examples to demonstrate the obvious folly of relying too heavily on Biblical literalism, before dismissing Dr. Jacobs. Sorkin was aware of the Internet letter before using it as fodder for the president's lines.

EPISODE: 26

EPISODE TITLE: *In This White House*
ORIGINAL AIR DATE: Wednesday, October 25, 2000
WRITTEN BY: Aaron Sorkin (teleplay), Peter Parnell, and Allison Abner
DIRECTED BY: Ken Olin
GUEST STARS: Emily Procter as Ainsley Hayes; Zakes Mokae as President Nimbala; Ted McGinley as Mark Gottfried
ALSO STARRING: Nicole Robinson as Margaret; Melissa Fitzgerald as Carol; Kim Webster as Ginger

SUMMARY

Sam gets lambasted on a TV talk show by a fledgling young Republican and Bartlet is so impressed he hires the woman; an American pharmaceutical company and representatives of an African country meet at the White House to talk about affordable AIDS medication; C.J. may have leaked important information to a reporter.

This episode marked the introduction of Ainsley Hayes, the junior Republican counsel who dominates Sam on a political talk show to such an extent that Bartlet decides to give her a job at the White House. The hiring had a precedent in real life — Sorkin cribbed the character from real-life young Republicans like Ann Coulter and Laura Ingraham who were popular faces on the talk-show circuit at the time. And he based the treatment that Ainsley gets after walking into the Democratic lion's den — the basement office, getting lost with nobody to show her around — on a memo written for him by Dee Dee Myers about what would happen in a real-life hiring.

The Ainsley character represents an unmitigated force of American patriotism. As a member of the opposing party, it's natural that the other staffers would feel some resentment towards her, and that she would be able to find flaws in their political positions. But as Sorkin himself told *George* magazine, she "has an extraordinary sense of duty. When her President asks her to serve, she agrees. Which makes her perfect for us." Ainsley is Sorkin's way of once again re-establishing a Capra-esque sense of pride in America — and American-style democracy.

EPISODE: 27

EPISODE TITLE: *And It's Surely to their Credit*
ORIGINAL AIR DATE: Wednesday, November 1, 2000
WRITTEN BY: Aaron Sorkin (teleplay); Kevin Falls and Laura Glasser (story)
DIRECTED BY: Christopher Misiano
GUEST STARS: John Larroquette as Lionel Tribbey
ALSO STARRING: Stockard Channing as Abby Bartlet; Emily Procter as Ainsley Hayes; Nicole Robinson as Margaret; Melissa Fitzgerald as Carol; Kathryn Joosten as Mrs. Landingham

SUMMARY
We meet White House Counsel Lionel Tribbey, Ainsley's new boss; Donna and the President work on a radio address; C.J. tries to stop a retiring military general from defaming Bartlet; and Ainsley has her first unpleasant experience working for the Democrats.

Played by John Larroquette, the multiple Emmy-award winning actor best known for his role on the long-running series *Night Court*, White House Counsel Lionel Tribbey made only one appearance on *The West Wing*. But it was a memorable one — Larroquette brought his signature forceful presence to the role, and viewers could only hope that they'd get a chance to see the character again.

The episode was also a real acid test for Ainsley, and even though Tribbey seemed as if he had a heart of stone, he comes to her aid when she really needs it. The scene in which Ainsley returns to her basement office and discovers the dead flowers with a "BITCH" notice on them is one of the most chilling scenes on the show so far. When Tribbey (with the help of Sam) fires the two young politicos responsible, he dismisses them with a curt "You two can go write your book now" — an obvious reference to the parade of "kiss and tell" biographies that always seem to follow the firing of DC political operatives. The episode's unifying theme is the staff's attempts to recall Gilbert & Sullivan trivia — the episode's title is a line from one of their operettas — and the staff throw Ainsley an office-warming party to the strains of a G&S overture.

EPISODE: 28

EPISODE TITLE: *The Lame Duck Congress*
ORIGINAL AIR DATE: Wednesday, November 8, 2000
WRITTEN BY: Aaron Sorkin (teleplay), Lawrence O'Donnell Jr. (story)
DIRECTED BY: Jeremy Kagan
GUEST STARS: Eugene Lazarev as Vassily Kononov
ALSO STARRING: Timothy Busfield as Danny; Emily Procter as Ainsley Hayes; Nicole Robinson as Margaret; Devika Parikh as Bonnie

SUMMARY
A Ukrainian politician shows up drunk and demands an audience with Bartlet; the staff tries to pass a test-ban treaty; and Donna presses for ergonomic legislation to make the nation's workplaces safer.

The highlight of this episode is Bartlet's encounter with the Ukrainian politician Vassily Kononov, who has arrived unannounced and inebriated at the White House and is demanding to see the President. Since he isn't an official representative of his country, Bartlet is not supposed to receive him according to diplomatic protocol. The staff must now contend with a drunk Ukrainian politician who won't take no for an answer.

The idea for this was based on an actual event and came from Marlon Fitzwater, a Republican advisor to real-life Presidents George Bush and Ronald Reagan. Fitzwater had been hired on by Sarkin as a consultant at the beginning of the second season. The real-life event involved Boris Yeltsin, who was challenging Mikhail Gorbachev for leadership of Russia, and wanted to meet President Bush. The White House staff had to come up with a compromise. Since Bush could not meet Yeltsin in the Oval Office because that would offend Gorbachev, a meeting was set up between the two in the national security advisor's office.

Bartlet arranges a similar compromise with Kononov; the Ukrainian gets to meet the President, and the administration gets to say that he was never allowed into the Oval Office. Another great example — this one supplied by a Republican! — of a real life event being woven into a fictional show.

EPISODE: 29

EPISODE TITLE: *The Portland Trip*
ORIGINAL AIR DATE: Wednesday, November 15, 2000
WRITTEN BY: Aaron Sorkin (teleplay), Paul Redford (story)
DIRECTED BY: Paris Barclay
GUEST STARS: Charley Lang as Congressman Matt Skinner
ALSO STARRING: Timothy Busfield as Danny; Emily Procter as Ainsley Hayes; Nicole Robinson as Margaret; Melissa Fitzgerald as Carol

SUMMARY
After making a crack about Notre Dame (Bartlet's alma mater), C.J. discovers

she has to accompany the President on a long plane trip; Sam and Toby have a difficult time writing a speech; Josh is confounded by a gay Congressman who won't oppose a bill banning same sex marriages; Leo's divorce papers arrive and the staff is afraid he might start drinking again.

Viewers hadn't seen a good substance-abuse story line in a while, but one of the episode's main subplots made up for it. Back in season, viewers saw that Leo had to overcome all his personal demons just to do his job: his political rivals were trying to expose his former alcoholism and drug dependence, his wife left him because he'd admitted his job was more important than his marriage, and his daughter was dating one of his staff.

Luckily for fans of the crusty McGarry, actor John Spencer carries off the part of the beleaguered Leo with tenacity and his own brand of self-deprecating charm. Many staffers (most notably, his assistant Margaret) think that the finality of receiving his divorce papers will be too much for the Chief of Staff, and begin to worry he will fall off the wagon. But as Leo says, in a line delivered in Spencer's trademark deadpan wit: "I'm an alcoholic. I don't need a reason to drink."

The episode is not all somber worrying about Leo, though. Sheen gets the opportunity to expand yet another side of the Bartlet character — his undying devotion to the Notre Dame Fighting Irish football team. When C.J. makes an offhand remark about the team, Bartlet "punishes" her by hauling her off to the West Coast with him. The sight of Allison Janney forced (on Bartlet's orders) to wear an ill-fitting green baseball cap while briefing the press corps is one of the show's high points in absurdity so far.

EPISODE: 30

EPISODE TITLE: *Shibboleth*
ORIGINAL AIR DATE: Wednesday, November 22, 2000
WRITTEN BY: Aaron Sorkin (teleplay), Patrick Caddell (story)
DIRECTED BY: Laura Innes
GUEST STARS: F. William Parker as the Rev. Al Caldwell; Annie Corley as Mary Marsh; Deborah Hedwall as Josephine McGarry; Henry O as "Chinese Refugee"
ALSO STARRING: Nicole Robinson as Margaret; Melissa Fitzgerald as Carol; Kathryn Joosten as Mrs. Landingham; Devikah Parikh as Bonnie

SUMMARY

The President must deal with 83 Chinese refugees fleeing persecution; two turkeys take up residence in C.J.'s office as Thanksgiving approaches; and Toby tries to persuade Bartlet to nominate Leo's sister to a high-profile education position.

A feature of *The West Wing* has always been the ability of the Sorkin team to switch back and forth between serious political drama and light-hearted comedy — a device used to near perfection in "Shibboleth."

On the one hand, Bartlet has to deal with the boatload of Chinese refugees who claim they are Christians persecuted in their homeland for their religious beliefs. This supplies the episode with all the drama it needs — Bartlet has to figure out whether the refugees are telling the truth about their religious beliefs, or just using this as a means of getting into the U.S. The solution that Bartlet ultimately devises, it should be noted, drew heavy criticism from TV pundits who believed that the resolution of the crisis was far too simplistic.

On the other hand, the fact that the White House was being overrun by turkeys (the feathered variety) injected an equally heavy dose of humor into the episode — especially when Bartlet has to come up with a presidential pardon for the birds so that they don't end up as centerpieces on a Thanksgiving Day dinner table.

The contrast between drama and comedy within the same one-hour format is likely one of the reasons *The West Wing* has remained so popular throughout the show's first two seasons. There just aren't that many prime-time shows that regularly juxtapose serious discourse with witty banter — and even fewer that would allow barnyard fowl to take on a significant role in plot development.

EPISODE: 31

EPISODE TITLE: *Galileo*
ORIGINAL AIR DATE: Wednesday, November 29, 2000
WRITTEN BY: Aaron Sorkin and Kevin Falls
DIRECTED BY: Alex Graves
GUEST STARS: Colm Feore as Tad Whitney; Charlotte Cornwall as Russian Ambassador
ALSO STARRING: Nicole Robinson as Margaret; Melissa Fitzgerald as Carol; Kathryn Joosten as Mrs. Landingham; Allison Smith as Mallory O'Brien

SUMMARY
Bartlet confronts the Russian ambassador over a fire in a missile silo; Charlie leaks word that the President does not like green beans; Bartlet prepares for a TV appearance with school kids as a NASA probe reaches Mars.

It's a testament to the success of *The West Wing* that there are very few scenes in the 40-plus episodes that aired in the show's first two seasons that fell flat. This episode has the dubious distinction of containing the only truly bad scene in a *West Wing* show so far. It appears in the middle of Bartlet and Leo's grilling of the Russian ambassador over a potentially disastrous fire in a Russian missile silo. The ambassador, played by guest star Charlotte Cornwall, steadfastly denies there is a problem, while the President and Chief of Staff keep up the pressure. Still, she maintains there is no problem.

Finally, Bartlet has had enough. With the kind of righteous indignation only Sheen can muster (the scene is OK up until this point) he asks her how she could ever have the gall to lie to them like that. Cornwall waits a beat and then delivers the scene-killing line: "From a long, hard Russian winter."

Ugh! For one thing, it's highly unlikely that a hard-nosed 21st-century diplomat would suddenly start sounding more like a poet than a politician, and it's completely out of character for the part. And for another, the line, by its very banality causes the scene to grind to a halt and expire like an over-wrought Dostoyevskian death-bed scene.

EPISODE: 32

EPISODE TITLE: *Noel*
ORIGINAL AIR DATE: Wednesday, December 20, 2000 (* this episode was scheduled to air on NBC on December 13, but was pre-empted by the Al Gore/George W. Bush speeches. In Canada, it aired on the CTV network as scheduled on the 13th, but was pushed back to the 20th on NBC)
WRITTEN BY: Aaron Sorkin (teleplay), Peter Parnell (story)
DIRECTED BY: Thomas Schlamme
GUEST STARS: Adam Arkin as Dr. Stanley Keyworth; Yo Yo Ma as himself
ALSO STARRING: Melissa Fitzgerald as Carol

SUMMARY
Josh gets counseling following some disturbing antics; cellist Yo Yo Ma performs at the congressional Christmas party; an Air Force pilot has an accident in an F-16; and a White House visitor makes an identification on a painting with symbolic importance.

It had been several weeks since the season-opening double episode, where we learned that Josh was most seriously wounded and profoundly affected by the shooting. Until this episode, though, it was not clear whether Josh would make a full and complete recovery. Due to a series of accidents and very strange behavior, he is forced, against his will, to get counseling.

One of the unshakable (until now) elements of the Josh Lyman character is his self-confidence and assurance bordering on arrogance. It's a testament to Bradley Whitford's acting ability that he was able in this episode to drop those defense after a long and difficult session with psychiatrist Dr. Stanley Keyworth, played by the veteran actor Adam Arkin. The two characters spend much of the first half of the episode verbally fencing with one another — Josh doesn't feel that he needs professional help while both Dr. Keyworth and Leo McGarry (who hired the psychiatrist) are convinced he does.

It's only through a series of well-crafted flashback scenes that viewers were able to discover what had been eating at Josh since the shooting. There's the obvious physical trauma, but Whitford had been playing the part for several episodes in a way that suggested Lyman's problems weren't just physical. For example, he seems to be over-identifying with an AWOL Air Force pilot and no one really knows why.

Sorkin and his team make excellent use of the music supplied by guest cellist Yo Yo Ma to bring the story of Josh's recovery to its profound conclusion.

EPISODE: 33

EPISODE TITLE: *The Leadership Breakfast*
ORIGINAL AIR DATE: Wednesday, January 10, 2001
WRITTEN BY: Aaron Sorkin (teleplay), Paul Redford (story)
DIRECTED BY: Scott Winant
GUEST STARS: Felicity Huffman as Ann Stark; Corbin Bernsen as Congressman Shallick
ALSO STARRING: Nicole Robinson as Margaret; Melissa Fitzgerald as Carol; Kim Webster as Ginger

SUMMARY
Toby is one of the few staffers who takes a two-party breakfast meeting seriously

— he gets burned by a counterpart in the Republican party; Josh and Sam set a near-disastrous fire in the White House; Leo and Toby decide that it's time to start planning for Bartlet's re-election.

At this point in the season, more than a few critics and chat room denizens were starting to suggest that Sorkin was recycling ideas from his short-lived *Sports Night* series. Whether the criticism was justified or not, he did recycle one of the major talents from his earlier series in this episode.

One of them was actress Felicity Huffman, in the role of the Republican Party Chief of Staff Ann Stark, who'd also played the role of Dana, one of the producers on *Sports Night*. When Toby insists on talking about "real" political issues at a bi-partisan breakfast meeting that everyone else is treating as a symbolic event, Stark feeds one of his offhand comments to a Republican party official to use against the Democrats later in a televised report.

The scenes with Huffman and Schiff are adroitly played by both sides — one is never quite certain whether they hate one another or respect each other as worthy foes. When he discovers he's been had, Toby is livid — he confronts Stark, who in turn is absolutely unapologetic; it's all part of the game for her. In a strange way, Toby seems to understand this. It's a shame we don't get to see Huffman again — her character provides an excellent rival for Toby Zeigler and their acerbic exchange gave the show one of its best moments of all-out Democratic vs. Republican antipathy.

The "staff as Three Stooges" theme is once again dusted off in the sub-plot, in which Josh and Sam try to set a fire in a fireplace that hasn't been used for years. It's another *West Wing* irony that the same men who can direct national policy and write brilliant speeches appear equally capable of burning down a national landmark through their bumbling carelessness.

EPISODE: 34

EPISODE TITLE: *The Drop In*
ORIGINAL AIR DATE: Wednesday, January 24, 2001
WRITTEN BY: Aaron Sorkin (teleplay), Lawrence O'Donnell Jr. (story)
DIRECTED BY: Lou Antonio
GUEST STARS: David Graf as Colonel Chase; Rocky Carroll as Cornelius Sykes; Roger Rees as Lord John Marbury
ALSO STARRING: Renée Estevez as Nancy; Kathryn Joosten as Mrs. Landingham; Nicole Robinson as Margaret; Melissa Fitzgerald as Carol; Kim Webster as Ginger; Devika Parikh as Bonnie

SUMMARY

Lord John Marbury returns, this time as the U.K. ambassador to the U.S.; Leo pushes for the development of a missile-shield defence system; C.J. has to persuade a comedian not to perform at an annual dinner; and Sam and Toby craft a speech for the President to deliver to the Global Defence Council.

Throughout the series, much time is devoted to scenes in which staffers — Sam and Toby in particular — are seen working away on speeches, mostly for the President. In fact, speech writing is Sam's major job, and on a number of occasions, Toby has held forth on the art and craft of speech writing.

An integral part of Bartlet's public speaking style is his easy ability to ad lib during a speech — the so-called "drop-in" that gives this episode its title. From early on, we've seen that one of Bartlet's major skills as a political speaker is his ability to hold an audience in the palm of his hand. In this episode we get an inside look at how these speeches are put together and the internal political dynamic that this activity generates. In the following two linked episodes, speech writing and delivery would take on a huge importance, so it's likely that Sorkin wanted to develop the whole oratory system within the staff before moving on.

It would be a disservice not to mention the return of Roger Rees in the role of Lord John Marbury in this episode as well. This time, his status has been upgraded from British diplomat to the U.K. ambassador to the U.S. And any time you get Marbury in on the action, it's a sure bet that Leo will be nearby to take a little abuse from the sharp-tongued aristocratic Brit. Why do Sorkin and the other writers continually subject a good guy like Leo to humiliation at the hands of Marbury? In this case, Leo's embarrassment is further compounded by the fact that a missile-shield defence system that he has been championing simply doesn't work, a fact eloquently expounded with evident glee by Marbury.

EPISODE: 35

EPISODE TITLE: *Bartlet's Third State of the Union* (part one of two)
ORIGINAL AIR DATE: Wednesday, February 7, 2001
WRITTEN BY: Aaron Sorkin (teleplay), Allison Abner, and Dee Dee Myers (story)
DIRECTED BY: Christopher Misiano
GUEST STARS: Corbin Bernsen as Congressman Shallick; Ted McGinley as Mark Gottfried; Richard Riehle as Officer Sloane
ALSO STARRING: Stockard Channing as Abby; Emily Procter as Ainsley Hayes; Marlee Matlin as Joey Lucas; Bill O'Brien as Kenny; Kathryn Joosten as Mrs. Landingham; Melissa Fitzgerald as Carol

SUMMARY

After much work by the staff, Bartlet delivers his most important speech yet, one which Leo, Toby, and Sam have crafted to signal his bid for re-election; Abby is enraged at her husband's apparent decision to run again; Josh and Joey Lucas struggle with a power failure at a polling center; C.J. loses her pants on national TV; a police officer being decorated for honorable service has a controversial past; and Leo and Bartlet must deal with five DEA officials kidnapped in Colombia.

Whew! Sorkin and crew seemed determined to pack as much drama as they could into the first half of this two-part story. The main story culminated in a huge argument between Abby and Jed Bartlet — the First Lady thought she had extracted a promise from the President that he would not seek re-election, but the night's speech has made it clear he had reneged on his promise.

Throughout the first two seasons Stockard Channing has done a remarkable job playing Abby Bartlet, but in this episode, she outdoes herself. In the key confrontation scene, which takes place in a kitchen over a gleaming stainless steel food prep table, she takes him to task for breaking his promise — and he responds just as hotly. Their argument ends prematurely though, because the President must do something about five drug enforcement agents who have been take hostage in Colombia. This emphasizes one of the key aspects in this relationship: Abby Bartlet realizes that her husband is married in equal parts to her and to his job, so she's prepared to put their argument on hold so the President can deal with the Colombian crisis. Time and time again, it's Abby who has to make those decisions. Although she's far from being the deferential politician's wife, she also realizes that marital disputes sometimes have to take second place behind the business of running a country.

EPISODE: 36

EPISODE TITLE: *The War at Home* (part two of two)
ORIGINAL AIR DATE: Wednesday, February 14, 2001
WRITTEN BY: Aaron Sorkin, Lawrence O'Donnell Jr., and Patrick Caddell
DIRECTED BY: Christopher Misiano
GUEST STARS: Tony Plana as Secretary of State; Ed Begley Jr. as Senator Seth Gilette; Ted McGinley as Mark Gottfried; Richard Riehle as Officer Sloane
ALSO STARRING: Stockard Channing as Abby; Emily Procter as Ainsley Hayes; Marlee Matlin as Joey Lucas; Bill O'Brien as Kenny; Kathryn Joosten as Mrs. Landingham

SUMMARY

Bartlet sends in a commando team to rescue the five hostages, but discovers the kidnapping was a set-up; C.J. gets the possibly disgraced cop an interview to explain his side of the story; the President and his wife discuss the medical implications of his running for re-election; Ainsley embarrasses herself in front of Bartlet for a second time.

Things had been getting pretty serious during the previous episode, so Sorkin and crew decided to inject some comic relief into the second part. In this episode Republican counsel Ainsley Hayes ends up slightly drunk and dancing around in her bathrobe in front of the President and then becomes trapped inside Leo's closet, hampering Sam's attempts to introduce her to the President so he can congratulate her on doing a good job so far.

The choice of Ainsley for the comic moments was an interesting one. Emily Procter plays the part with a blitheness that makes her an easy character to get flustered when things don't go right — she has that Sam/Josh/Toby/C.J. syndrome of being extremely bright and very good at her job but prone to outbreaks of ineptitude. Procter also has this endearing habit of acting as though she might burst into tears at any moment. That's also a good quality for registering embarrassment, which she does on two profound occasions in the dual episodes.

Speaking of emotions, critics have often noted that one of the most compelling that Sheen displays regularly as Bartlet is a hair-trigger temper. In this one, the Bartlet anger is at its hottest, when he discovers that nine American agents have been killed trying to resolve the fake kidnapping in Colombia. It may be only acting, but Sheen must be able draw on some powerful emotions to get so mad so fast.

EPISODE: 37

EPISODE TITLE: *Ellie*
ORIGINAL AIR DATE: Wednesday, February 21, 2001
WRITTEN BY: Aaron Sorkin (teleplay), Kevin Falls, and Laura Glasser (story)
DIRECTED BY: Michael Engler
GUEST STARS: Mary Kay Place as Surgeon General Millicent Griffith; Kathleen York as Congresswoman Andrea Wyatt; Nina Siemaszko as Eleanor "Ellie" Bartlet
ALSO STARRING: Nicole Robinson as Margaret; Melissa Fitzgerald as Carol; Kim Webster as Ginger; Kathryn Joosten as Mrs. Landingham; Renée Estevez as Nancy

SUMMARY

The president's middle daughter tells the press that her dad would never fire the Surgeon General, who's made controversial comments of her own about the legalization of marijuana; Toby asks for his ex-wife's help in recruiting a new member to a Social Security panel.

It had been a while since we'd seen Zoey Bartlet, and an equally long time since we'd seen Bartlet in his role as a father. This episode included both, with the appearance of Nina Siemaszko as Eleanor "Ellie" Bartlet, after whom the episode was named. Siemaszko had appeared in *The American President* in 1995, but this was the first time we'd met Bartlet's middle child on *The West Wing*.

The episode brought to light one of the real-life problems with being a child of the President, namely, that it's hard to have a normal life outside the media spotlight. As recent events with George W. Bush's daughters illustrate, every little step (or misstep) they take comes under scrutiny by a headline-seeking media, and when they really mess up, the exposure can be severe and unrelenting.

In the fictional world of *The West Wing*, Ellie Bartlet hasn't done anything as serious as drinking under the legal age, but she does go on record as defending Millicent Griffith, the Surgeon General (played by guest star Mary Kay Place) who had just made comments about the legalization of pot on an online chat forum that were so controversial that Bartlet had asked Leo to demand her resignation. Ellie tells the press that there's no cause for concern — her dad and Griffith are old friends and that he'd never fire her.

In addition to illustrating the pressures on a First Kid and a parent who happens to be the President when it comes to media scrutiny, the episode also gave us some insight into Bartlet's relationship with his offspring. In his interaction with Zoey, Bartlet had been protective but fair — he knew his daughter was experimenting with college life and did his best to keep a low profile as she and Charlie began a relationship. But with Ellie, Bartlet feels considerable guilt that he does not know his middle daughter better. In the end, he intends to come down hard on her for her indiscretion in talking to the press but he can't quite do it. The interaction between the two suggests that Sheen — who, after all, has children of his own — knows a thing or two about when a father should pull his punches.

EPISODE: 38

EPISODE TITLE: *Somebody's Going to Emergency, Somebody's Going to Jail*
ORIGINAL AIR DATE: Wednesday, February 28, 2001
WRITTEN BY: Aaron Sorkin and Paul Redford
DIRECTED BY: Jessica Yu
GUEST STARS: Roma Maffia as Officer Rhonda Sachs; Jolie Jenkins as Stephanie Galt
ALSO STARRING: Nicole Robinson as Margaret; Anna Deveare Smith as National Security Adviser Nancy McNally; Melissa Fitzgerald as Carol; Kim Webster as Ginger

SUMMARY

On the second annual "Big Block of Cheese Day" the White House is again open to all comers; Sam helps a friend of Donna's investigate her grandfather's past as a possible spy; Toby makes a speech to World Trade Organization protesters where he meets a cop who seems to be his female doppelganger.

A great episode for fans of Sam Seaborn/Rob Lowe. Using the plot device of Sam agreeing to help Donna's friend to obtain information about her grandfather's possible involvement in wartime espionage, writers Sorkin and Redford get another chance to remind us why Sam is a such a valuable character on the show — as a die-hard patriot, he's constantly in pursuit of the clear-cut, constitutionally-approved way of solving problems. That is, until his conscience reminds him that the "right" way is not always the best way. In the same way that Sam knew that continuing to see Laurie was a bad move but still kept on doing it, in this episode, he uncovers information about the grandfather that proves he was a spy, and yet (at Donna's urging) he tells the friend he was not able to find anything — his conscience won out over his rational mind.

In fact, it's almost as though Sorkin returns to the character of Sam when he wants to remind us that amidst all the high-pressure wheeling and dealing that goes on in the show, the characters can still make decisions based on personal feelings. Speaking of feelings, the show's final scene does a great job of re-affirming Sam's humanity. After getting a big hug from Donna for not blowing the whistle on the spy/grandfather, the two are met by an ebullient Josh, who informs them that Toby has just given a killer speech at the WTO protest — and the group is going out to celebrate. But Sam hangs back — he has to call his father, who he earlier learned had been guilty of marital infidelity. In the same way as he found it in his heart to "pardon" the wartime spy for the sake of his granddaughter, Sam "pardons" his dad by giving him a call. The episode ends with the line from the Don Henley song, *In a New York Minute*, that provided the installment's title.

EPISODE: 39

EPISODE TITLE: *The Stackhouse Filibuster*
ORIGINAL AIR DATE: Wednesday, March 14, 2001
WRITTEN BY: Aaron Sorkin (teleplay), Peter McCabe (story)
DIRECTED BY: Bryan Gordon
GUEST STARS: George Coe as Senator George Stackhouse
ALSO STARRING: Tim Matheson as Vice President Hoynes; Melissa
Fitzgerald as Carol

SUMMARY

*An elderly Senator launches into an impromptu filibuster and nobody knows
why; Bartlet tells Leo at dinner that he's promised Abby he wouldn't run again;
Hoynes stuns Toby by agreeing to fight the energy sector; and C.J. has lost a gift
given to Bartlet by the president of Egypt.*

Instead of relaying the numerous plots in this episode the usual scene-by-
scene way, Sorkin and McCabe use the device of having C.J., Josh, and Sam
write e-mails to their parents, telling them about what has been going on in
their lives. Lots of viewers may have been getting out their dictionaries to
remind themselves of what a "filibuster" is, but the point came across clearly
enough — the 78-year-old Senator Stackhouse wanted, for some reason, to
block progress in the Senate, and did not care if it was a holiday weekend
when people were rushing to get out of town.

Just what was his reason for doing it? Donna won praise from the other
staffers when she discovered that Stackhouse had an autistic grandchild. It
seemed reasonable this had something to do with the filibuster and not (as
Bartlet had suspected) because the President had not attended Stackhouse's
wife's funeral. Even though Donna's "discovery" was a little transparent, using
it to end Stackhouse's filibuster was pretty classy as it allowed the aged
senator to depart with his dignity intact.

A key subplot in the episode revolved around a crucial scene between Ziegler and Hoynes, because it marked the first time Toby began to wonder about Bartlet's health. You had to know that someone as shrewd as Toby would eventually clue in that something was up with the president; when Hoynes assures Toby that what he knows about the inner workings of the party would stun him, you could just feel the air go out of him — a rare occurrence for someone more accustomed to being on the other end of shocking statements like that. Instead of confirming once again that Hoynes was a virtual outsider when it came to determining party strategy, it had the exact opposite effect — now Toby was starting to think that maybe he was the one on the outside.

EPISODE: 40

EPISODE TITLE: *17 People*
ORIGINAL AIR DATE: Wednesday, April 4, 2001
WRITTEN BY: Aaron Sorkin
DIRECTED BY: Alex Graves
ALSO STARRING: Emily Procter as Ainsley Hayes

SUMMARY

Toby broods about Hoynes's comments regarding the secrets he knows and approaches Leo; when told about Bartlet's MS *he erupts in anger about not having been informed earlier; Josh and Donna quibble over their "anniversary"; Josh, Sam, Donna, and Ainsley work to make a Bartlet speech funny.*

The theme of Toby as the ultimate-insider-turned-outsider continues in this episode, with Richard Schiff playing to perfection the brooding, contemplative communications director who knows something is up but isn't sure what. Schiff is especially effective in bringing out that side of the character that's sullen one moment and instantly emotional the next — when the

President tells him about his MS, Tony instantly calculates (in typical Toby fashion) the potentially disastrous consequences of keeping it hidden, and lashes out at the riskiness of it all. And Sheen, in full confessional mode, plays a Bartlet who turns the other cheek, gently reminding Toby that despite the political consequences, there is also a life at stake here — his.

The episode also revisits another recurring plot line — the potential Donna–Josh romance. It's significant here because of the banter between them throughout the episode concerning the day the two started to work together — what Donna likes to call their "anniversary." Whitford and Moloney really know how to act their way around a will-they-or-won't-they relationship, and this episode contains some of the best subtly tense moments between the two so far. While neither actor gives any of their character's true feelings away, they're not doing much to rule out the possibility there might be something interesting brewing after all.

EPISODE: 41

EPISODE TITLE: *Bad Moon Rising*
ORIGINAL AIR DATE: Wednesday, April 25, 2001
WRITTEN BY: Aaron Sorkin (teleplay), Felicia Wilson (story)
DIRECTED BY: Bill Johnson
GUEST STARS: Oliver Platt as White House Counsel Oliver Babish; Jacqueline Kim as Lieut. Emily Lowenbrau
ALSO STARRING: Emily Procter as Ainsley Hayes; Nicole Robinson as Margaret; Melissa Fitzgerald as Carol; Kim Webster as Ginger; Kathryn Joosten as Mrs. Landingham; Devika Parikh as Bonnie

SUMMARY
A new White House counsel confronts the problem of Bartlet's non-disclosure of his medical condition, while the staff rush to solve various crises.

Jed and Sam: long-time screen presences Sheen and Lowe gave The West Wing *the star power it needed when it first launched in September 1999*

The advance buzz on this one was that *Bad Moon Rising* would mark the introduction of guest star Oliver Platt, in the role of the White House counsel Oliver Babish, for a four-episode stint that would run to the end of the season.

Platt, who movie fans recognized from films like 1993's *The Three Musketeers* and 1998's *Bulworth*, also starred in a short-lived (it lasted only six episodes) TV series called *Deadline*, where he played an abrasive, drink-sodden New York tabloid columnist. In real life, Platt had started doing his homework on the Babish character and the Washington political scene at an early age — his father was a career diplomat who'd held a number of over-seas government postings.

One of the great things about the way Sorkin develops characters on *The West Wing* is how he's able, in one short scene, to allow viewers to find out all they need to know about how a character is going to handle situations from then on. The way we discovered that Platt's Babish character was a no-nonsense, straight-ahead kind of guy was one of the single greatest scenes in any show to date. When we first meet Babish he's fooling around with a tape recorder that, presumably, he uses to tape interviews with his clients. He's also joking with a secretary about a judge's gavel he likes to keep on his desk.

When Bartlet starts to tell him why he's come to see him — that he may need to put together a defence against possible impeachment — Babish pauses briefly, then slams the gavel down onto the recorder, wham! Talk about keeping comments off-the-record. And talk about brilliant timing in a scene.

In another typical example of character work by Sorkin, Bartlet — who's less than eager to meet the new counsel — tells Leo that lawyers like Babish are always reminding him that he's not a lawyer, and besides, he's sure that Babish doesn't even play chess. Later, when we see the two talking for the first time in Babish's office, the camera moves in toward them — showing a wooden chess set in the foreground. Did Babish put it there before the meeting, knowing the President was a fan of the game, or is he a chess player himself? We never find out — but it was a nice touch.

When Babish finishes with Leo and Bartlet, viewers are left with a big question — how will the other members of the White House staff hold up under his pressure-cooker questioning style? Clearly, this is a guy who's so straightforward and focused, he barely has time for the obligatory deference and politeness expected when dealing with the President. What's he going to do with wise guys like Josh and Sam, or someone easily flustered like C.J., when he doesn't have to stand on ceremony? And is Babish really the kind of guy you want defending you in the crunch? He's no hand-holder, but maybe that's just the kind of person you want in your corner when the opposition is trying to prove you've committed fraud against an entire country.

EPISODE: 42

EPISODE TITLE: *The Fall's Gonna Kill You*
ORIGINAL AIR DATE: Wednesday, May 2, 2001
WRITTEN BY: Aaron Sorkin (teleplay), Patrick Caddell (story)
DIRECTED BY: Christopher Misiano
GUEST STARS: Oliver Platt as White House Counsel Oliver Babish; Lee Wilkof as Martin Conelly

ALSO STARRING: Marlee Matlin as Joey Lucas; Nicole Robinson as Margaret

SUMMARY
The Babish inquisition continues as the rest of the staff gets the news about Bartlet's MS*; Josh hires Joey Lucas to conduct a fake poll to see how the President would do in an election; Toby finally gets over not being told sooner; and Donna is duped by a fax that predicts the imminent crash of a Chinese satellite.*

Early in the life of the series, Aaron Sorkin was sometimes accused of creating women characters who were often frailer and less assertive than their male counterparts. He countered by saying that he objected to the supposed need for women's parts in film and TV to be extra-strong and continually dynamic. What's wrong with a woman character with the same frailties as the average male character — and on *The West Wing* one could argue that *all* the male characters are frail or flawed to some degree.

C.J. Cregg is one of these frail-but-convincing woman characters. Throughout the show, Allison Janney has played the press secretary with just the right mix of humor, assertiveness, and general confusion. Although she is adept at controlling the media, she is just as likely to fall off a treadmill or in a pool, or appear on national TV without pants. Consequently, fans wanted to see how Sorkin would portray her taking the news of Bartlet's MS. In the end, C.J. was the was one staffer who seemed to be the hardest hit by the news. The knee-jerk reaction would be to criticize Sorkin for having her, as the only woman among the senior staff, take the news the hardest. But that reaction ignores a basic law of good TV writing — characters should act as you'd expect them to act, given their past experiences. C.J. takes the news the hardest not because she is female, but because of all the main staffers, she's the one viewers expected would react that way.

When she's trying to reach down for some powerful emotion in a scene, Janney will often touch a large scar on her leg, and one could surmise she was compelled to touch it several times during the scenes when she struggles to come to terms with Bartlet's news. Eventually, in later episodes Janney was able to pull her character back under control, but for now a frazzled C.J. was the C.J. viewers had come to know and love.

Viewers had to wonder, given her current state of mind, how C.J. would hold up under Babish's relentless questioning.

EPISODE: 43

EPISODE TITLE: *18th and Potomac*
ORIGINAL AIR DATE: Wednesday, May 9, 2001
WRITTEN BY: Aaron Sorkin (teleplay), Lawrence O'Donnell Jr. (story)
DIRECTED BY: Robert Berlinger
GUEST STARS: Stockard Channing as Abby; Oliver Platt as White House Counsel Oliver Babish
ALSO STARRING: Marlee Matlin as Joey Lucas; Bill O'Brien as Kenny; Anna Deveare Smith as National Security Adviser Nancy McNally; Nicole Robinson as Margaret; Melissa Fitzgerald as Carol; Kathryn Joosten as Mrs. Landingham; Devika Parikh as Bonnie

SUMMARY
Counsel Babish continues his relentless questionings and warns Abby about possibly serious consequences to her if there's an investigation; the President and his team try to decide in secret meetings how to break the news of his MS to the nation; the staff still doesn't know if Bartlet will run again; the U.S. is forced to respond to a coup in Haiti; and Mrs. Landingham is killed.

Despite the plethora of plot lines swirling around this episode, *18th and Potomac* will likely be remembered as the one in which Mrs. Landingham died.

Her death is totally unforeseen. Throughout the episode, Kathryn Joosten, who played Mrs. L. with just the right amount of old-school charm and down-to-earth wit, was masterful in portraying a woman who knows that given the fact that she is a senior citizen and a woman, she is going to get a lot of unsolicited advice from men about purchasing her first new car. Bartlet alludes to her New England thrift in relying on used vehicles in the past, and Mrs. Landingham has adamantly refused to take advantage of her position to try and get a discount on her new set of wheels.

But even as Dulé Hill is taking the final phone message informing him that Mrs. Landingham was killed when a drunk driver smashed into her while she was on her way back to show the staff her purchase, it is hard to realize that tragedy has struck. Part of the problem comes from the fact that Sorkin and co-writer Lawrence O'Donnell crammed the episode full of action and sub-plots, including the crisis in Haiti and the continuing thread about Bartlet's disclosure of his MS and his decision whether or not to run again for president. It's an interesting question exactly why Sorkin decided to kill off a popular character at the tail end of a busy season in an already-chaotic episode, especially since it didn't involve a real-life contract dispute or anything similar.

Whatever the answer, for the many fans who had come to love Mrs. Landingham's frequent appearances during the show's first two seasons, it was a tragic way to end her involvement in the series.

EPISODE: 44 (SEASON TWO FINALE)

EPISODE TITLE: *Two Cathedrals*
ORIGINAL AIR DATE: Wednesday, May 16, 2001
WRITTEN BY: Aaron Sorkin
DIRECTED BY: Thomas Schlamme
GUEST STARS: Stockard Channing as Abby; Oliver Platt as White House Counsel Oliver Babish
ALSO STARRING: Nicole Robinson as Margaret; Anna Deveare Smith as National Security Adviser Nancy McNally; Melissa Fitzgerald as Carol; Kim Webster as Ginger; Kathryn Joosten as Mrs. Landingham; Kristen Nelson as the young Mrs. Landingham

SUMMARY

The President and staff attend the funeral of Mrs. Landingham; Bartlet gathers his top military advisers for a strategy session on the Haitian conflict; the President's disclosure of his medical condition airs to the nation; Mrs. Landingham appears and offers some ghostly advice; we learn all about how Bartlet and Mrs. Landingham joined forces in flashback sequences where we also meet Jed's father.

Critical opinion on the 2000–01 season finale was mixed — many felt that Sorkin relied too heavily on the clichés of TV drama and used too many obvious plot tricks, like the cursing of God in Latin, the crushed-out cigarette on the church floor, and the ghostly flashback scenes with Mrs. Landingham.

You'd have to be a pretty innocent TV-watcher (or a big Sorkin fan) not to admit that the ending hands-in-pockets scene was pretty well telegraphed by the comments of the young Mrs. L in the flashback scene about 25 minutes from the end. Likely still feeling the sting of criticism from last season's cliffhanger finale, Sorkin ended this one with just a little bit of mystery about Bartlet's re-election plans, but given a few of the messages earlier in the episode, his decision seemed pretty clear.

Still, no matter what you thought about most of the episode, it was hard not to be moved by its final five minutes, almost all of which transpired with no dialogue, and only the strains of the Dire Straits song "Brothers in Arms" playing quietly as background. Sorkin included a number of symbolic gestures in the final sequence, including Charlie leaving his raincoat off in solidarity with the President who was refusing to wear one in spite of the downpour, and the President's refusal to answer a C.J.-planted soft question to lead off his press conference. It was also a nicely-understated touch that despite all the buildup surrounding the televised admission of his MS in the prior episode, we only got to hear the program on CNN as background on a TV set in another scene.

The Mrs. Landingham flashback scenes were interesting from the overall point of view of the show's development, but Sorkin and crew had used returns to the past extensively throughout the first two seasons, so there was no surprise there. But the ghostly-apparition scenes were something new. Before the 2001–02 season began, Kathryn Joosten explained to TV critics in Toronto that she had recruited Kristen Nelson, the young actress that ended up playing her part as a young woman, having worked with her on other projects. Landingham read her lines into a tape recorder so that Nelson could go over them repeatedly to get the older woman's voice down just right. Joosten also added that although she wasn't exactly sure how the whole thing would work out, she did know that there were plans to bring Mrs. Landingham back as a spectral visitor in future episodes.

SOURCES

Interviews:

Friend, Tad (via telephone, New York City). 4 Apr. 2001.

Gayle, Lesley. Webmaster, "Testytoads" West Wing site
    (http://www.testytoads.com/TWW), via e-mail. Feb.–Apr. 2001

Janney, Allison, Rob Lowe, Richard Schiff, Martin Sheen, John Spencer, Bradley
    Whitford, Thomas Schlamme, Aaron Sorkin, John Wells. NBC Summer
    Press Tour, Pasadena, California, 29 July 29 1999 (transcript).

Kohanik, Eric. Hamilton, Ontario, 12 Mar. 2001.

Nix, Susannah. Webmaster, "Inside the Bartlet West Wing" site
    (www.jedbartlet.com), via e-mail. Feb.–Apr. 2001.

Schiff, Richard, Dulé Hill, Kathryn Joosten. CTV Fall Press Tour, Toronto, Ontario, 5
    June 2001.

Sorkin, Eric (interviewed by Eric Kohanik). NBC Winter Press Tour, Pasadena,
    California, Jan. 2001 (transcript).

Vagt, Rachel. Webmaster, "TKTV" West Wing site (http://thewestwing.tktv.net), via e-
    mail. Feb.–Apr. 2001

Warne, B.E. Webmaster, "The West Wing Continuity Guide"
    (http://westwing.bewarne.com/), via e-mail. Feb.–Apr. 2001.

Whitford, Bradley and Janel Moloney. NBC Summer Press Tour, Pasadena, California,
    19 July 2000 (transcript).

Web Sites:

EpGuides.com: http://www.epguides.com/westwing
Inside the Bartlet White House: http://www.jedbartlet.com
The Internet Movie Database: www.imdb.com
The West Wing *Continuity Guide*: http://westwing.bewarne.com
MightybigTV: www.mightybigtv.com
NBC *Media Village*: http://www.nbcmv.com
NBC's *Official* West Wing *Site*: www.nbc.com/westwing
Testytoads West Wing *Site*: http://www.testytoads.com/TWW
This Week on the Left . . . er West Wing:
        www.geocities.com/the_left_wing/main.html
TKTV's West Wing *Site*: http://thewestwing.tktv.net

Articles:

Allemang, John. "West Wing action now speaks louder than words." *Globe and Mail*, 18 Oct. 2000, p. 2.

Adansom, Rondi. "Hey! That looks like Kristin holding the gun . . . J.R.'s sister-in-law strikes again." *National Post*, 4 Oct. 2000, p. E3.

Ballerstero, Dana. "Best Part: The Sheen Shine." *Hispanic*, July–Aug. 2000, p. 36.

Belcher, Walt. "It's a landslide Emmy win for 'West Wing' over 'Sopranos.'" *Tampa Tribune*, 11 Sept. 2000, p. 1.

Billin, Andrew. "Perpetual Spin: Andrew Billen settles into the West Wing of the White House." *New Statesman*, 14 Feb. 2000, p. 46.

Bobbin, Jay. "Beating around the Bush: Life goes on for Bradley Whitford and the cast of *The West Wing*." *TV Times*, 12 Jan. 2000, p. 6.

—. "High Notes: W.G. Snuffy Walden has made beautiful music for some of TV's top shows." *TV Times*, 14 Apr. 2000, p. 4.

Branegan, Jay. "You Could Call It the Wonk Wing: NBC's hit White House series has become a national civics lesson." *Time*, 15 May 2000, p. 82.

Brioux, Bill. "*West Wing* Shocker: Tonight's the night we learn who gets hit in that explosive *West Wing* finale." *Toronto Sun*, 4 Oct. 2000, p. 55.

Carson, Tom. "Comfort Food: TV's tastiest fantasy is *The West Wing*." *Esquire*, May 2000, p. 66.

Chang, Yahlin. "TV's Top Dogs: Brand-name television creators are dominating the new season — Aaron Sorkin and John Wells are two of the hottest." *Newsweek*, 11 Oct. 1999, p. 80.

Cushman, Robert. "Nice Guys get elected." *National Post*, 4 Oct. 2000, p. E7.

Feschuk, Scott. "The President takes a trip. *The West Wing*'s finale tasted strongly of mushrooms." *National Post*, 18 May 2001, p. B3.

—. "Genius even in the silences: *The West Wing* proves that TV can approach high
    art." *National Post*, 6 Apr. 2001, p. B5.

Feuerherd, Peter. "A 'Wing' and a Prayer." *Commonweal*, 10 Mar. 2000, p. 47.

Fitzwater, Marlin. "The Right Wing Joins the *West Wing*." *People*, 6 Nov. 2000, p. 26.

Franklin, Nancy. "Corridors of Power: Spin doctors and damage control in the
    White House." *New Yorker*, 21 & 28 Feb. 2000, p. 290.

Friend, Tad. "Laugh Riot: What happens when a newcomer tries to bend the rules
    of the most vulnerable and conservative of cultural forms — the
    American sitcom?" *New Yorker*, 28 Sept. 1998, p. 76.

Gliatto, Tom; Leonard, Eizabeth. "A Second Chance: His Brat Pack misadventures
    behind him, Rob Lowe, sober, grown-up and grateful, savors family life
    and the surprising success of *The West Wing*." *People*, 11 Sept. 2000, p. 112.

Goldstein, Patrick. "On a Wing and a Prayer: *Sports Night* and *West Wing*
    creator/writer Aaron Sorkin is flying by the seat of his pants as he strives
    for perfection on both shows." *L.A. Times*.

Gordan, Ben. "Bang! Bang! Shots in the Dark: Who got shot? The season premiere
    tonight of *The West Wing* has the answers." *National Post*, 4 Oct. 2000, p.
    E6.

Govani, Shinan. "Now, a message from the Washington Tourist board: The city is
    nothing like the TV version of the U.S. capital." *National Post*, 4 Oct. 2000,
    p. E2.

Hamilton, Kendall, Yahlin Chang, Corie Brown, Debra Rosenberg. "Coast to Coast:
    Two buzzed-about TV shows go behind the scenes in Hollywood and
    Washington. Get ready for the wild tales of two cities." *Newsweek*, 6 Sept.
    1999, p. 64.

Johnson, Brian D. "White House Hustle: Liberal Fantasy thrives in *The Contender*
    and *The West Wing*." *Maclean's*, 16 Oct. 2000, p. 70.

Keveney, Bill. "Down to the last detail: Carefully crafted *West Wing* admired by all
    on the set." *National Post*, 4 Oct. 2000, p. E1.

King, Joshua. "Do You Recognize the Clinton West Wing in *The West Wing*?"
    Atlantic Monthly, online edition, Mar. 2001.

Kohanik, Eric. "Hail to the Chief: It's that thoughtful, honest leader who draws us
    to *The West Wing*." The Watcher, *Post TV*, 3 Nov. 2000, p. 5.

L.A. Times online staff. "TV Writer Charged in Drug Case." *L.A. Times*, online
    edition, 1 May 2001.

Lee, Luaine. "Channing's *West Wing* role suits her wanderlust." *Minneapolis Star
    Tribune*, 5 May 2000, p. 10E.

Lehman, Chris. "The Feel-Good Presidency: The pseudo-politics of *The West Wing*."
    Atlantic Monthly, Mar. 2001, p. 93.

Lewis, Robert. "The Answer to *West Wing* Withdrawal." *Maclean's*, 29 May 2000. p. 2.

Lippman, Laura. "The Lovable Liberal Behind Bush's Victory." *New York Times*, 31 Dec. 2000, p. 28.

Littlejohn, Cynthia. "*West Wing*'s Sorkin pleads guilty to drug charges." *Hollywood Reporter*, online edition, 20 June 2001.

Lowry, Brian, Louis Sahgun. "*West Wing* Creator Arrested in Drug Case." *L.A. Times*, online edition, 17 Apr. 2001.

McKissack, Fred. "*The West Wing* is not a Wet Dream." *Progressive*, May 2000, p. 39.

Morris, Dick. "*The West Wing* got it all wrong. Former Clinton strategist says it's far sneakier in real life." *National Post*, 4 Nov. 2000, p. A1.

National Post staff. "A humble Aaron Sorkin honoured for *West Wing* work." *National Post*, 10 May 2001, p. B14.

National Post staff. "We need more suspense; let's put the space shuttle in peril: It's the drama, stupid." *National Post*, 4 Oct. 2000, p. E3.

Olbermann, Keith. "Man at his Best: The Tube. The showdown — *Sports Night*'s creator squares off with its inspiration." *Esquire*, June 1999, p. 24.

Ollove, Michael. "*West Wing*'s Bartlet is the President Voters Wish for Television: Chief executive of the popular NBC series has all the qualities anyone could want. And that is why the show fulfills viewers' fantasies." *Los Angeles Times*, 7 Nov. 2000, p. 3.

People staff. "Capitol Hill: Tap master Dulé Hill brings in 'da noise once again, with a breakthrough role on TV's *The West Wing*." *People*, 22 May 2000, p. 161.

—. "Taking Wing: Once too tall for Hollywood, Allison Janney now flies high on *The West Wing*." *People*, 3 Apr. 2000, p. 89.

Pierson, David. "*West Wing* Creator Pleads Not Guilty in Drug Case." *L.A. Times*, online edition, 3 May 2001.

Poniewozik, James. "Capital Ideas: A speechwriter's — sorry, scriptwriter's — D.C. series." *Time*, 4 Oct. 1999, p. 96.

Rose, Alex. "Can *West Wing* survive after Bill Clinton goes?" *National Post*, 4 Oct. 2000, p. E3.

Ryan, Andrew. "Corridors of Power: Getting behind the closed doors of politics on *The West Wing*." *Globe Television*, 16–22 Dec. 2000, p. 4.

—. "The Left Wing: He's a fictional prime-time president. But in his real-life guise of political activist, Martin Sheen talks with Andrew Ryan about Bush's drinking, Gore's thinking and the fate of the country's highest office." *Globe and Mail*, online edition, 15 Nov. 2000.

Schultz, Nancy. "The E-Files: Mad for Mulder? Got a Jones for Buffy? Juiced by JAG? In the Fanfiction Realm, You Can Make the Plot Quicken." *Washington Post*, 29 Apr. 2001, p. G01.

Smith, Terrence. "Online Focus: Aaron Sorkin." *Newshour Online*, 27 Sept. 2000.

Spencer, Miranda. "In the Spotlight: Martin Sheen." *Biography*, Jan. 2000, p. 18.

Tucker, Ken. "Diary of a Frazzled TV Writer." *Entertainment Weekly*, 2 Feb. 2000, p. 39.